THE FUTURE OF EMPLOYMENT
IN AFRICA

THE FUTURE OF EMPLOYMENT IN AFRICA

DEMOGRAPHY, LABOUR MARKETS AND WELFARE

LOÏC DE CANNIÈRE

ANTHEM PRESS

Anthem Press
An imprint of Wimbledon Publishing Company
www.anthempress.com

This edition first published in UK and USA 2025
by ANTHEM PRESS
75–76 Blackfriars Road, London SE1 8HA, UK
or PO Box 9779, London SW19 7ZG, UK
and
244 Madison Ave #116, New York, NY 10016, USA

British Library Cataloguing-in-Publication Data
A catalogue record for this book is available from the British Library.

Library of Congress Cataloging-in-Publication Data: 2025931862
A catalog record for this book has been requested.

ISBN-13: 978-1-83999-383-1 (Hbk) / 978-1-83999-384-8 (Pbk)
ISBN-10: 1-83999-383-9 (Hbk) / 1-83999-384-7 (Pbk)

Cover Credit: Cover art by Jirka De Preter - https://www.jirkadepreter.be

This title is also available as an e-book.

CONTENTS

LIST OF FIGURES

ACKNOWLEDGEMENT

Over the past 25 years, I have had the privilege of engaging with small entrepreneurs and farmers – both men and women – across more than 20 African countries. These experiences form the true foundation of my understanding of the continent. I am deeply grateful to them for the inspiration they have provided. Their resilience continually fuels my motivation and focus. It is truly remarkable to witness how individuals, often overlooked and without wealth, power or prestige, cultivate a sense of self-worth through the success of their small businesses. These individuals deserve the highest respect. I dedicate this book to them.

INTRODUCTION: AFRICA
IS NOT A COUNTRY

Africa is a huge continent, bigger in terms of land mass than China, India, the United States and Europe put together. Its 54 countries are very diverse in terms of their geography, language – around 2,000 languages are spoken – culture, religion and economy. So, I realise how risky it is to write about Africa in a way that might suggest the continent forms a coherent whole. The Nigerian journalist Dipo Faloyin even warned against this pitfall in the title of his book *Africa Is Not a Country*.[1]

I wrote this book out of concern, respect and friendship for Africa. As a European, it is not my place to make recommendations to Africans. I instead look to the future, keeping an open mind and drawing on my experiences in often extremely diverse countries on the African continent. I write from the perspective of an economist and based on my experience as an investor, having been involved in numerous impact investments – initiatives driven by passionate African entrepreneurs that provide ordinary people with access to decent work and life. My story is primarily about the daily lives of Africans, many of whom I have had the privilege of meeting, speaking to and working with over the last 25 years. Some have become friends for life. It is these encounters that form the real basis of my knowledge and passion for Africa.

Over the past decade, numerous publications have emerged about the (ongoing) injustice that has been done to Africa. They have helped fundamentally change our view of the continent, something that was desperately needed. In this book, I build on those findings to provide a clearer understanding of the reality of contemporary Africa. However, my primary focus is on the future, particularly the next 20 to 30 years. I am convinced that over the next three decades, as we approach 2050, there will be a fundamental change to the face of Africa. Population growth and jobs will play a decisive role here. How can Africa create a future with more prosperity and less poverty for all?

The evolutions in Africa will also have a profound geopolitical impact on the relationship with both Europe and the rest of the world. I will examine what role Europe can and should play in this.

We have compelling reasons to be optimistic about Africa. Contrary to the impression the media gives us about the situation in Africa, I am convinced that, in the coming decades, the continent will make itself heard in a positive way.

Bloody Civil War and African Humour

It is August 1998. I am 38 years old and setting foot on African soil for the first time. The golden emblem on my old, burgundy-coloured passport has since completely rubbed off. I am travelling to the Republic of the Congo (Congo-Brazzaville) on behalf of my employer, the Belgian marine engineering company DEME[2], to assess the Port of Pointe-Noire on the Atlantic coast for some potential dredging work. In my role at DEME, I help marine engineering clients with the financing of their projects. The concept of project financing also dates from that period. This is where large infrastructure works provide their own financing through their economic returns. For example, new ports or port expansions are financed by future port dues. Since the port authority of Pointe-Noire is short on cash, I have been sent out to help them come up with a feasible financing strategy.

At that time, the Republic of the Congo was just emerging from a bloody civil war between two claimants to the presidency: Pascal Lissouba and Denis Sassou Nguesso, a former army colonel who had come to power in 1979 following a military coup. In 1992, he had to hand over the reins to Pascal Lissouba, who had been democratically elected to the presidency. Denis Sassou Nguesso proceeded to join the resistance and then retook power by force in 1997, with the support of the French president – and his good friend – Jacques Chirac, as well as the support of Angola.

I landed in the capital Brazzaville to discover a city that had been largely destroyed. The stark contrast between the devastation and the breathtaking beauty of the Congo River rushing past was truly profound. The river boasts the second-largest water flow in the world, surpassed only by the Amazon. Where it flows past Brazzaville, the Congo is wide and mighty. Large branches, piles of grass, bushes and even trees whizz past in the brown water. From Brazzaville, you can make out – on the other side of the water – the Congolese capital Kinshasa, defined by the high-rise office blocks in the Gombe business district.

Many buildings in Brazzaville lay in ruins. All the streets had been torn up. The 106-metre-high Nabemba Tower, known as Elf Tower back then, had also suffered serious damage. Defining Brazzaville's skyline, this gold-coloured, futuristic-looking building, designed by French architect Jean-Marie Legrand, looks like a tall, thin pepper mill. The tower was built in 1992 with a loan from the French oil company Elf-Aquitaine to the Republic of the Congo. The repayment of the loan had been guaranteed with a pledge on future oil revenues from the Republic of the Congo to Elf-Aquitaine. I would later come to realise that such practices were commonplace. In 2003, Elf-Aquitaine merged with Total and the company is now called TotalEnergies.

For safety reasons, I had a chaperone for the duration of my stay in Brazzaville. One day while I was walking to a meeting in the city, he hurried me into a side alley out of harm's way. Two companies of around two hundred heavily armed Angolan soldiers ran past, shouting battle cries and thumping their black shiny boots on the ground. The soldiers were very tall and looked well-trained and strong. My chaperone advised me to steer clear of them at all times.

There were various stories doing the rounds about the presence of the Angolans. They had apparently supported the return of Denis Sassou Nguesso. Others said they remained on standby to cross the Congo River at any moment: after all, the Angolans had also played a major role in the departure of Congo's president Mobutu a year earlier and in the takeover of power by Laurent-Désiré Kabila. They were reportedly ready to support Kabila in the event of any problems.

One evening, I went in search of a restaurant in the city. Most places were closed due to the ongoing civil war, so I ended up in an old, dreary-looking building with a big dining room. There were about fifty large tables made of dark tropical wood. But otherwise, it was completely empty, like an echo of the precarious situation in the city. When I asked if I could have dinner, the waiter responded with: *Avez-vous réservé, Monsieur?* This was my first encounter with African humour and self-mockery.

Glaring Poverty

The following day, there were clear skies for my flight on an old DC-3 to Pointe-Noire, the Republic of Congo's second city. As we flew over the dense jungle between Brazzaville and the Atlantic coast, my fellow passengers told me that was where opposition militants were hiding and continuing to take armed action against Nguesso.

I visited the relatively small Port of Pointe-Noire, the entrance to which was partially blocked by a huge sandbank. A mountain of white, glistening sand rose a good 20 metres above sea level. For years, the port authority had not had the money to have the sandbank dredged. The port had only one dock, in the shape of a square, which was also directly connected to the sea on just one side. So the sandbank was narrowing the entrance to the dock – a real nightmare for the crews of ships coming into dock.

Pointe-Noire displayed fewer traces of the civil war than Brazzaville. But the glaring poverty was harder to miss. In between the shabby constructions stood a large Elf-Aquitaine compound surrounded by high concrete walls topped with barbed wire. This is where the company's expats lived.

To put together a budget for the dredging project, we organised a second trip to Pointe-Noire a few weeks later, this time with an engineer who would carry out the cost calculation. To estimate the cost, we had to collect data on the hardness of the material to be dredged and on the soil type in the dock. We had no choice but to rent a sloop to manually take samples from the bottom of the dock. We then travelled back to Belgium with these soil samples stowed away in small, waterproof containers in our hand luggage.

Based on the cost calculation, I drew up a financing proposal. However, it then turned out that the Republic of the Congo, despite being an oil exporter, no longer had any repayment capacity and therefore could not take out any more loans. The state, in collaboration with Elf-Aquitaine, had pledged all future oil revenues to Elf-Aquitaine and to European banks. It later turned out that it was President Denis Sassou Nguesso himself who, together with Elf-Aquitaine, had pledged the proceeds for the next 10 years. He had also diverted money to his own Swiss bank accounts. According to *Le Monde*, the French state and Elf-Aquitaine were closely involved in these financial constructions, in which Jacques Foccart, 'Monsieur Afrique' and adviser to President Chirac, played a major role.

Mental Turning Point

Over the years that followed, I regularly travelled to Africa on behalf of DEME. The only way to get large infrastructure projects in West Africa financed was with good agreements, a balanced financial plan, a good overview of cash flows and appropriate financing. This was how I gradually discovered the importance of good infrastructure projects for Africa, alongside appropriate and professional financing.

During that period, I also often travelled to India, Vietnam and the Philippines and, for example, helped finance a project to deepen the Gorai River in Bangladesh. The Gorai is a branch of the Ganges that provides irrigation to southwestern Bangladesh. Deepening the river was an important ecological project to resupply a valuable mangrove area with fresh water. We were able to secure the financing for the project thanks to a loan from the World Bank and a Belgian state-to-state loan.

During one of these work trips to Bangladesh, we took a boat trip on the Buriganga, which flows through the capital Dhaka. Along the riverbanks, I saw Bengalis working in pitiful conditions in tanneries, open-air smelters and shipyards. The women used handheld tools to break stones.

The trip on the Buriganga became a mental turning point for me. Increasingly, I started asking myself how people could gain access to decent work and how inclusive economic systems could be encouraged.

Focus on sub-Saharan Africa

In this book, I will highlight the dramatic poverty in sub-Saharan Africa by mapping out what determines that poverty and estimating how that situation could evolve from now until 2050. Put positively, I aim to look for opportunities to bring prosperity to all Africans. Distributed prosperity can only be achieved if there are enough decent jobs for everyone. I will point out the challenges, but also the signs of hope that justify my optimism.

I am driven by concern, respect and friendship for Africa – and by the realisation that Africa has suffered a lot of (ongoing) injustice. I find the view of the recently deceased and much-lamented Belgian Congo expert Kris Berwouts very inspiring. He always considered how he could engage with Africa in a non-patronising way, working with Africans as equals, and effortlessly inserting himself into an African structure without seeing himself and his white world at the top of it. How he could contribute to real change without making his own vision and values the norm.[3]

I would like to adopt the same attitude, but as an economist and investor. I aim to carry out well-substantiated analyses and promote impactful investments that provide more Africans with access to decent work and life.

For this, I have chosen to focus on sub-Saharan Africa because that is the region where poverty is most acute. So unless otherwise stated, 'Africa' always refers to sub-Saharan Africa, the countries south of the Sahara.

Where I do want to make recommendations is to the European political, economic and financial institutions, which I have inside experience of. Above all, I want to call on them to take action. Discussing Africa only in the context of the relatively marginal policy topic of development cooperation, or in terms of migration and border controls, is not enough.

Evolution of Poverty

Over the past 30 years, global extreme poverty has experienced a phenomenal decline. The World Bank considers people to be 'extremely poor' if they have an income of less than $2.15 a day.[4] Despite the growth of the world's population, the number of extremely poor people decreased from 2 billion to 712 million between 1990 and 2022.[5] The proportion of extremely poor people in relation to the entire global population decreased spectacularly from 37 per cent to 8 per cent,[6] mainly due to economic growth in Asia, especially in China and India. In contrast to the rest of the world, poverty in sub-Saharan Africa continued to increase over the same period, from 282 million in 1990 to 411 million extremely poor people in 2019.[7] In relation to the total population, extreme poverty is very high (36 per cent in 2019). Global poverty is therefore increasingly concentrated in sub-Saharan Africa. By 2030, around nine in ten of the world's poorest people will live in sub-Saharan Africa.[8] The continent will at that point have almost half a billion people classed as 'extremely poor'. Today, the poorest people on our planet are *mainly* African. In the coming decades, they will be *almost exclusively* African.

Poverty is a very complex phenomenon and one with many causes. People can get caught in a poverty trap for many reasons, like lack of work, adequate education, health care, nutrition or water. Or because of insecurity, violence and war, climate conditions, poor governance and exploitation and so on. Moreover, the causes of poverty can differ greatly from region to region. Living conditions in African cities differ significantly from those in the villages of the savannah. It is not my goal to capture the African poverty phenomenon in its entirety but rather to focus on the interaction between poverty and employment. More employment means less poverty. Conversely, a lack of jobs leads to more poverty. Therefore, creating more jobs is the best and most efficient weapon we have in the fight against poverty.[9]

Book Outline

In the first chapter, I take a closer look at the poverty figures in Africa and compare them with the rest of the world. Poverty and demography each influence one another. I look at the expected demographic growth in Africa for the next 30 years and try to estimate the consequences of this for employment. This is because employment determines income and prosperity, or lack thereof – and that is poverty. I then extend the analysis to the interaction between demography, employment and poverty on the one hand and migration and climate on the other. Employment, demography, climate and migration, together with poverty, form a pentagon of factors that all influence each other (see also the diagram in Chapter 1).

In the second chapter, I try to understand the root causes of the lack of prosperity in Africa. I reference authors who have conducted extensive and relevant research on this subject. Reading their analysis sheds light on the factors that have hindered wealth creation and contributed to poverty in the past, and that continue to do so today. This diagnosis helps us avoid prejudices and errors of judgement, make a better and more realistic assessment of the future, and focus on Europe's role and responsibility in this.

In the third chapter, I look to the future: at how and where in Africa more jobs and prosperity can be created for all Africans in the next 30 years. Jobs contribute to reducing poverty. But although this is an essential topic, there are very few publications that highlight the situation in Africa. Furthermore, the available analyses are often fragmented. That is why I am making my own assessment of how the African labour market could look in the coming decades. To do this, I rely extensively on what I have seen and learnt on the ground over the past 30 years.

In the fourth chapter, I describe Africa's economic dynamism from the bottom up and how this contributes to more employment and less poverty.

In the fifth and final chapter, I discuss the relationship between the European Union (EU) and Africa. I also look at China's position in Africa. There is a growing realisation within the European institutions that Europe must change its stance when it comes to its relationship with Africa. The policy steps taken by the EU in recent years are headed in the right direction. But there is still a lot of work to be done. Moreover, Europe is still looking for its specific role and place on the continent.

Getting My Boots Muddy

I write about Africa as an economist and as an investor. I am not a historian, professor of literature, anthropologist, political scientist or agricultural engineer. In writing this book, it is not my goal to provide an academically substantiated analysis of the African economy and society. My vision is based on what I have seen and experienced first-hand. Since the mid-1990s, I have regularly travelled through Africa. First for the Belgian marine engineering company DEME and since 2001 as a manager at Incofin, a social 'impact investor'[10] for the Global South.

In the year 2000, the impact investor and social investment company Incofin took out a newspaper advertisement looking for a South Manager. Incofin invests in small banks, agricultural and food companies and small-scale drinking water companies. The company's top priority is not profit, but rather financial sustainability and social-ecological impact for low-income people at the bottom of the pyramid. Its vision is to support a fair transition towards a sustainable economy where nobody is excluded.

I applied for the role and got the job. My task was to monitor and develop Incofin's investments in Africa and Latin America. Back then, Incofin was very small, so I was actually the only guiding force. Incofin had been founded 10 years earlier by vdk bank in Ghent and by a Belgian non-governmental organisation (ACT, now Trias). The advertisement caught my eye at the time because Incofin was doing exactly what I thought needed to be done: investing in business activities in developing countries so that people can work in decent conditions and improve their socio-economic situation.

DEME was also supportive of my career switch: if it did not work out, I could always return to my job at the marine engineering company.

Incofin has invested more than $450 million in Africa over the past 20 years, spread across 91 companies in 20 countries. Through our investments, we are able to reach more than 10 million African entrepreneurs (almost 1 per cent of the population of sub-Saharan Africa). Incofin is one of the world's larger impact investors, with almost a hundred employees, offices on five continents and investments amounting to $1.3 billion.

I have helped set up companies and sat on the boards of African enterprises, together with African directors and business leaders. Together we have shared both the risks and the opportunities. I have also had many intense conversations with them, including with their employees and their customers. I have never lived in Africa, but I have had the opportunity to explore many African countries and their diverse realities.

In the first few months of 2001, I visited Incofin's investments in Tanzania, Uganda, Guinea, El Salvador, Honduras, Guatemala and Brazil. In Guinea, Incofin had invested in small companies in the Kindia region, about 130 kilometres from the capital Conakry. The city left a poor impression on me. Its unpaved streets had formed an open sewer, leaving an unbearable stench of rotting fish and faeces hanging in the air. The level of poverty was unmistakable. However, Guinea is home to a third of the world's bauxite reserves (the raw material for aluminium). Guinea mines its reserves through the Compagnie des Bauxites de Guinée, 51 per cent of the shares of which are today held by Alcoa, Rio Tinto and Dadco. Despite this wealth, Guinea, like the Republic of the Congo, has never managed to use its natural resources for the benefit of its own people. When I visited the country, the president was Lansana Conté, an autocratic dictator who came to power following a coup in 1984. The people hated him because he did nothing for his country. I would later come across the same kind of attitude in the Congo, during the presidency of Joseph Kabila.

Not long before my trip to Guinea, two boys had been found frozen to death in a plane's cargo hold at Brussels airport: 14-year-old Yaguine Koïta and 15-year-old Fodé Tourikara. They were carrying a letter with a dramatic message for European leaders: 'Dear sirs, members and leaders of Europe. It is to your solidarity and kindness that we, in Africa, appeal. Help us. We are suffering enormously in Africa [...]: the war, the diseases, the food and so on. [...] Nevertheless, we want to study and we ask you to help us study so that we, in Africa, can become like you.'

A heart-wrenching letter... The boys had risked their lives in a desperate and dramatic attempt to improve their living conditions. This terrible event once again cut straight to the heart of the problem: African young people must be given the opportunity of an education and jobs in their own country.

When I started at DEME in 1995, I had just completed my career as cabinet chief for economic affairs of the Flemish prime minister. In this role, I was responsible for designing employment policy during a period of relatively high unemployment. The topic of decent work for everyone continues to fascinate me to this day.

When I left the cabinet, Marc Stordiau, the then CEO of DEME, sent me to work at a building site in Taiwan for three weeks as training. I lived on-site with the rest of the crew. Marc wanted me to 'get my boots muddy'. Otherwise, I would never properly understand the company. When I left for Taiwan, he told me to hold the dredged sludge in my hands and smell it. It was excellent advice. I spent a great deal of time on board of the dredging vessel and learnt a lot: about dredging, about the pumps, about the engines, about the hardness of the subsurface, about the wear of the cutter teeth, about the pipelines and the dredging dump, about the lives of the crew members. You learn so much from the reality on the ground.

Years earlier, I had befriended a colleague whose grandfather had served as governor of the Société Générale de Belgique, a renowned holding company from colonial times that once held significant stakes in the Congolese copper and cobalt mining industry. He had given me some similar advice: 'The only way to understand the reality is to start from the bottom up.' I try to use that same approach in Africa, Latin America and Asia. That view from the bottom up has also made me very critical of policy plans that are developed and implemented from the top down.

My many encounters with small entrepreneurs and farmers on the ground, from the bottom up, form the real basis of my knowledge. They keep my motivation and drive focused. It is wonderful to see 'unimportant' people without any money, power or prestige gain a sense of self-worth by successfully building up their own small business. These people deserve the utmost respect.

Notes

1 Dipo Faloyin, *Africa Is Not a Country – Breaking Stereotypes of Modern Africa* (Harvill, 2022).
2 DEME is a leading company specialised in dredging, marine infrastructure, environmental works and offshore energy. https://www.deme-group.com.
3 Kris Berwouts, *Mijn leven als mushamuka: schetsen van Rwanda, Burundi en Congo* (Epo, 2020), 260.
4 The World Bank defines 'extremely poor' as people with an average income of less than $2.15 a day (at 2017 purchasing power parity figures).
5 The World Bank, Poverty and Inequality Platform. Accessed 31 December 2024. https://pip.worldbank.org/poverty-calculator.
6 Ibid.
7 2019 is the most recent number for sub-Saharan Africa. Admittedly, poverty in sub-Saharan Africa did decrease in relative terms (from 54 per cent in 1990 to 36 per cent in 2019), mainly as a result of rapid population growth.
8 World Bank Blogs, 'Projecting Global Extreme Poverty Up to 2030: How Close Are We to World Bank's 3% Goal?'. Accessed 31 December 2024. https://blogs .worldbank.org/opendata/projecting-global-extreme-poverty-2030-how-close -are-we-world-banks-3-goal. The estimate still uses the previous definition of 'extreme poverty', that is, an income of $1.90 a day at 2011 purchasing power parity figures.
9 Louise Fox and Melissa Sekkel Gaal, *Working Out of Poverty: Job Creation and the Quality of Growth in Africa* (The World Bank, 2008). https://docu-ments.worldbank.org/en/publication/documents-reports/documentdetail /316891468212385709/working-out-of-poverty-job-creation-and-the-quality -of-growth-in-africa.
10 Impact investments are investments that aim to achieve both a financial and a positive social-ecological return.

CHAPTER 1

THE PROSPERITY PENTAGON

The so-called prosperity pentagon can help us gauge the evolution of poverty in Africa over the next 30 years. It is made up of five factors that all influence each other: poverty, demography, employment, migration and climate (Figure 1). These are the ingredients of a complex interaction that determines the creation of prosperity and the fight against poverty.

In this chapter, I shed light on these five factors and their impact on the future. In doing so, I also look beyond the borders of the African continent because issues like migration and climate disruption, of course, have global implications.

Poverty

Over the last 25 years, I have made many trips to India, for both DEME and Incofin. This is a country where I have witnessed shocking and abject poverty, in both the cities and the countryside. But during those years I have also seen the impressive transformation of the Indian subcontinent. New roads have appeared everywhere, and the infrastructure has been improved by building factories, schools and hospitals. Extreme poverty in India has significantly decreased: from close to 50 per cent of the population in 1993 to 13 per cent according to the latest available figures.[1] More than 260 million Indians have been able to escape extreme poverty since 1993.[2] But there is undoubtedly also a dark side to the Indian story.[3] The income distribution in the country has become increasingly unequal: the richest 10 per cent earn almost 60 per cent of the national income, almost twice as much as in the 1980s.[4] This economic growth has also been accompanied by a dramatic increase in greenhouse gas emissions, with India becoming the third-largest emitter after China and the United States. Between 1990 and 2020, emissions increased by 335 per cent.[5]

FIGURE 1 The prosperity pentagon.

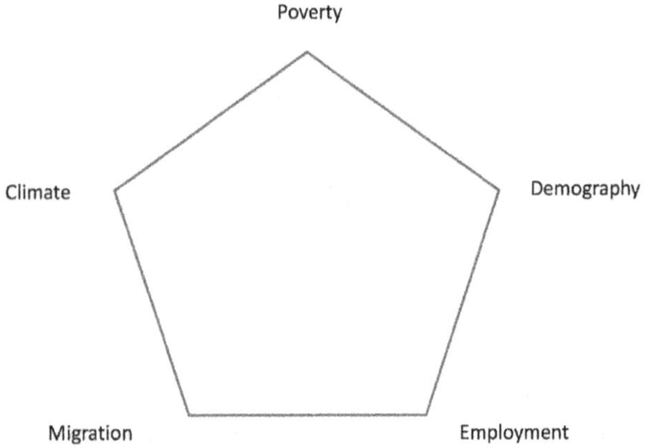

Furthermore, the country is also flirting with a dangerous and potentially violent religious nationalism.

In that same period, Africa has taken a very different path. Between 1990 and 2019, extreme poverty in sub-Saharan Africa increased from 282 to 411 million people. While India spent those 30 years lifting 400 million people out of extreme poverty, Africa added over 100 million to its statistic. As already mentioned, by 2030 more than eight in ten of the world's poorest people will live in sub-Saharan Africa.

Not only is the proportion of extreme poverty in Africa very pronounced, but the average standard of living is also much lower than in the rest of the world. The average annual income per capita increased from $3,348 in 1990 to $4,309 in 2023.[6] Meanwhile, over the same period, the average annual income worldwide increased from $11,262 to $20,670.[7] While global per capita income grew by 83 per cent over the last 33 years, the average annual income in Africa increased by only 28 per cent. African income today is about one-fifth of the global average. The national income (GNI) of the entire sub-Saharan Africa (1.1 billion inhabitants) is equal to that of Germany (83 million inhabitants).

Admittedly, income per capita is far from a perfect indicator. As a parameter, it tells us nothing about how those incomes are distributed, about the negative effects of growth (for example, due to environmental damage) or about other important elements related to quality of life.[8] It is therefore a limited parameter, but one that does provide an indication of the income disparities or the economic vulnerability of the lowest earners.

Ghana versus South Korea

The economic evolution of, for example, Ghana and South Korea over the last 50 years also nicely illustrates how growth patterns can differ greatly between countries on separate continents. In 1957, right after Ghana's independence and at the end of the Korean War, the per capita incomes of Ghana and South Korea were on a par.[9] In 1991, more than thirty years later, economics professor Hans Werlin observed that the per capita income in South Korea was 10 times higher than in Ghana. I made the same calculation again based on 2023 World Bank figures and found that the gross national income (GNI) per capita has since increased to $6,796 in Ghana compared to $50,572 in South Korea.[10] In other words: 66 years on, the per capita income in South Korea is still more than seven times higher than in Ghana. This is despite the fact that Ghana, at the time it became independent, was a very prosperous country, partly due to its extensive export of gold and cocoa to Europe. South Korea, meanwhile, was left devastated at the end of the Korean War. Ghana pursued a policy of import substitution, choosing to manufacture products itself rather than import them. But this was not successful, partly due to an unstable political climate (with several coups). South Korea instead opted for the development of an export industry, starting out with less sophisticated products like wigs before expanding to heavy industry and shipbuilding.

Different growth patterns

In the same way that Africa is not one country, it also does not have one economy. Instead, its economies vary considerably from country to country. Belgian professor Stefan Dercon carried out extensive research into the differences between economic growth patterns of African countries and found two that managed to halve extreme poverty between 1990 and 2018: Ethiopia and Ghana. For a decade before the Covid-19 pandemic, Ethiopia was the fastest growing economy in the world.

Rwanda and Botswana are also on the list of fastest growing economies. In contrast, there are seven countries where extreme poverty more than doubled between 1990 and 2018: Angola, the Congo, Kenya, Madagascar, Malawi, Nigeria and Zambia.[11]

Dercon also tries to explain the causes of these growth differences, so I will come back to his analysis in Chapter 2.

The significant income differences are not limited to *between* African countries. Income differences, in fact, also increased *within* African countries. In the last 30 years, an African middle class of approximately 350 million people has emerged.[12] They can be found in big cities like Nairobi, Maputo and Lagos. This middle class is relatively prosperous, well educated and has strong purchasing power, making it a source of growth for the continent. However, I will instead focus on the almost 400 million Africans at the bottom of the socioeconomic pyramid.

Demography

Demographic developments in Africa are crucial for gaining insight into future employment and prosperity – or lack thereof.

In 2020, sub-Saharan Africa had 1.2 billion inhabitants, as many as the entire European continent and North America put together.[13] Over 60 years, the African population increased fivefold, which means an average population growth of more than 2.5 per cent per year. Never before in the history of the world have we witnessed a faster population growth than this.[14] The average annual population growth in Europe over the same period was just 0.3 per cent.

The population explosion in Africa since 1960 can be explained by two factors: an increase in life expectancy and a persistently high birth rate. Demographers predict that population growth in Africa will continue for decades to come because not only is life expectancy continuing to rise, but the birth rate is also declining much more slowly than on other continents.

Life expectancy has increased from 40 years in the 1960s to 60 years today.[15] This evolution is mainly due to the reduction of infant mortality, brought about by better health care for young mothers.

The birth rate peaked in the 1970s and 1980s, when women gave birth to an average of six children (Figure 2). In other parts of the world, including the rest of the Global South, the birth rate declined during that period. In Africa, the birth rate only started to decline slowly and to a limited extent from the 1990s onwards. Today, African women have an average of 4.6 children, compared to European and North American women, who have 1.5 children.[16]

According to the UN's 2022 population projections, the birth rate in subSaharan Africa will remain higher than on other continents. But it is true that the birth rate in Africa is already showing a downward trend. From 2050, the birth rate is predicted to drop below three children per woman. In the rest of the world, birth rates are expected to remain roughly stable in the coming decades. And by the end of this century, the birth rate in Africa should be almost equal to the global average.

FIGURE 2 Evolution of the birth rate in sub-Saharan Africa compared to the global average. Source: © United Nations, DESA, Populations Division. Licensed under Commons Creative CC BY 3.0 IGO. United Nations, DESA, Populations Division, World Population Prospects 2022 (http://population.un.org/wpp) – CC BY 3.0 IGO.

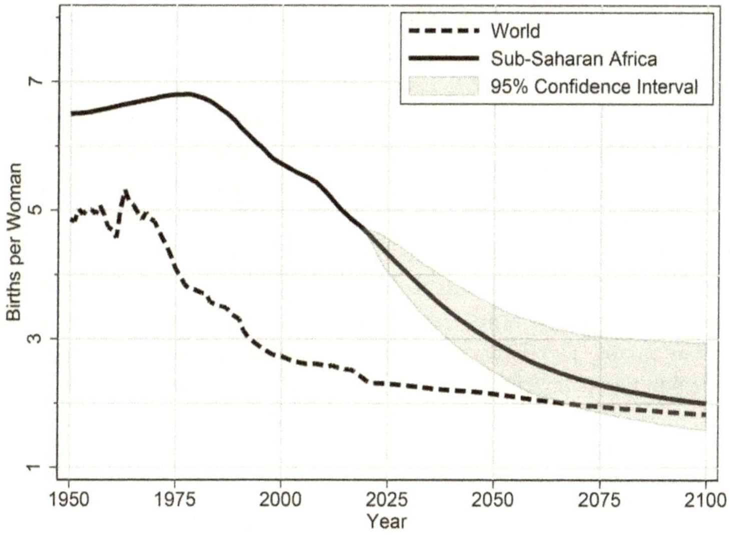

The UN estimates that the population of sub-Saharan Africa will increase to 2.1 billion people by 2050 and to 3.4 billion by 2100.[17] These projections are based on assumptions about life expectancy, birth rate and net international migration flows. In reality, of course, these parameters can evolve in a different way than what was predicted. This is why the projections always indicate a confidence interval (shown on a fan chart) that gets bigger the further into the future the predictions extend. As a comparison, the population projections for the EU are 423 million inhabitants by 2050 and 349 million by 2100. This means that, while the African population will significantly increase, the EU population will decrease. By 2050, there will be almost five Africans for every European. In 2100, that ratio will increase to ten to one.

Figure 3 illustrates the historical and UN-expected population evolution per continent.[18] Note how over the course of the current decade (2020–2030), the population of sub-Saharan Africa is set to overtake the combined population of Europe and North America, before continuing to rise for several decades to come. From 2050, Africa will become far and away the region with the largest population in the world. Meanwhile, the populations of Europe and North America will stagnate or even continue to decline.

According to the UN's median projection, the world's population will increase by 1.8 billion people (from 8 to 9.7 billion) from now until 2050. Africa will account for half of this growth (0.9 billion).

However, the UN's projections are being questioned by some specialists.[19] They challenge the UN's deterministic, mechanistic calculation method and introduce more qualitative determinants, like the influence of general education on birth rate (the better the access to education, the lower the birth rate) and health care. While the UN assumes that the global population will steadily increase until the end of the twenty-first century, these demographers believe that – in the baseline scenario – the world's population will peak at 9.7 billion people in 2064 and then decline to 8.7 billion in 2100.[20] This is a difference of 1.6 billion people in 2100 compared to the latest UN projections. Furthermore, they believe that if the entire population of sub-Saharan Africa would have access to secondary education and contraception by 2030 – in line with the UN Sustainable Development Goals – the African population would reach only 1.5 billion people by 2100, less than half the UN estimate. But as long as infant mortality remains high and people have no confidence that at least some of their children will survive, the birth rate will also remain high.

FIGURE 3 Evolution of the global population per region (in billions). Source: United Nations, DESA, Populations Division. World Population Prospects 2022, own graph based on 'GEN/01/REV1: Demographic indicators by region, subregion and country, annually for 1950–2100'.

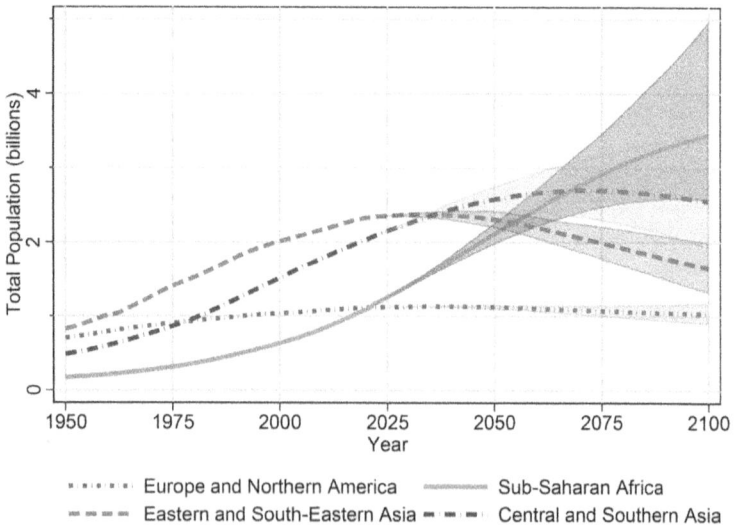

Employment

Africa has a very young population. More than half are younger than 25 years old (61 per cent of the population in 2022[21]). According to UN estimates, the number of young people will increase by half as much again by 2050 (from 719 million young people in 2022 to 1.1 billion in 2050[22]). This means there will be roughly 400 million more young people in Africa over the next thirty years. And the working population (aged 15–64) will grow by 670 million people.

The demographic evolution in Africa has important consequences for the labour market. If these UN projections are correct, an average of 23 million additional jobs per year will be needed in Africa to absorb the growth in the working population (15–64 years) between 2022 and 2050.[23]

This need for jobs due to the increase in young people is a huge challenge for the continent. If Africa is unable to provide jobs for these young people, there will be serious repercussions for the income of Africans, resulting in poverty and a lack of prosperity.

This demographic explosion can also be seen as an opportunity. While other continents are facing an ageing and stagnating workforce, for the next 30 years Africa can benefit from a young and growing workforce. And from 2034, Africa will have a larger working population than China.[24] This offers growth opportunities for the continent.

The demographic evolution in Africa is accompanied by an increase in urbanisation. In 2018, 42 per cent of Africans lived in cities. According to UN estimates, that figure will rise to 59 per cent by 2040.[25] In absolute numbers, the urban population in Africa will triple: from 548 million people in 2018 to 1.5 billion in 2050. Nowhere in the world will there be so many people living in cities. The Congolese capital Kinshasa is expected to become the most populous city in the world by 2075.[26] And from 2100, Lagos in Nigeria will become the world's largest city with an estimated 88 million inhabitants.[27]

Of course, you may wonder whether these projections are realistic: won't people prefer to avoid these kinds of megalopolises in the future? Fundamentally, this rapid urbanisation is the result of two phenomena: firstly, natural population growth remains very high (approximately 2.5 per cent) and secondly, the rural population is migrating to the cities in search of a better future. Belgian professor Baudouin Michel from the University of Kinshasa (UNIKIN) investigated this phenomenon for Congo.[28] He found that population growth in Kinshasa is more than 6 per cent per year: made up of 2.5 per cent natural population growth and more than 3 per cent growth due to rural migration to the cities. He organised a series of interviews in Congolese villages to understand why villagers migrate to the city, identifying three reasons: they think they will find better health care in the city, they hope their children will get an education there and they see no future for themselves in the countryside. However, Kinshasa (and other African megacities) are not ready to accommodate an annual population growth of 5 to 6 per cent. The roads, water supply and sewerage systems, education and health infrastructure cannot keep pace with the growth. This situation will only lead to even more misery and poverty for the population in the *cités* of Kinshasa. Mass unemployment (or menial jobs) among young people will lead to tensions, turning cities into hotbeds of social unrest.

As we just saw, the birth rate in Africa has started to decline. Demographers expect that trend to continue in the coming decades, albeit only slowly. As a result of the demographic transition, the ratio of the inactive population (under 15 and over 65 years) to the active working population (15–64 years) is decreasing. That ratio is called the dependency ratio. A declining dependency ratio means that the group of non-active people (children and the elderly) that are dependent on the active population is shrinking. This phenomenon can lead to an increase in macroeconomic prosperity – known as a demographic dividend. This is what happened in East Asia between 1960 and 1990, and partly explains the economic miracle experienced there.[29] The UN estimates that the dependency ratio in sub-Saharan Africa will decrease from 79 per cent in 2023 to 58 per cent in 2050 and even to 53 per cent in 2100.[30] However, a demographic dividend does not automatically lead to greater prosperity. For this, various conditions need to be met, like an economic environment that makes job creation possible. I will look at the possible opportunities for job creation later on.

Migration

There is a link between demography, poverty and migration – the fourth dimension in our prosperity pentagon. A rapidly growing young African population (with the need for tens of millions of new jobs each year) could put pressure on and disrupt the local labour market and education system. A lack of jobs and education would, in turn, put young people at risk of ending up in poverty. This can then trigger *intra*continental or *inter*continental migration flows.[31] However, it is very difficult to predict the direction and magnitude of future migration flows.

A remarkable experience with Ethiopian transmigrants

In the summer of 2018, I received a phone call from Pieter Demeester, the son of a former Belgian minister. He wanted to know whether I was familiar with economic networks in Ethiopia and would be willing to help him work out how to set up a meaningful business project in Ethiopia. The goal was to help a group of Ethiopian migrants who had ended up staying with him and his family, having exhausted all legal avenues to remain in the country. Socially conscious Pieter and his wife, Olivia Vanmechelen, live with their children in Brussels. Since Incofin had invested in the Ethiopian microfinance institution Wasasa – I knew the management team well and had met them in Ethiopia – I was happy to help Pieter. And it turned out to be a remarkable experience.

During the migration crisis, there were hundreds of refugees living in appalling conditions in Maximilian Park, opposite the Immigration Office (DVZ) in Brussels. At that time, the DVZ was unable to cope with the influx of applications, only managing to register a limited number of asylum applications a day. The refugees, therefore, stayed as close as they could to the DVZ to make sure they were first in the queue every morning. On top of that, they had nowhere else to sleep, so were camping in tents in the park.

The first major takeover of Maximilian Park took place in 2015 during the Syrian crisis. The park then experienced another large influx in 2018 when a huge number of transmigrants from all over attempted to reach Great Britain.

In February 2018, Pieter and Olivia – after weighing it up with their children for several months – decided to offer shelter to two refugees and so registered themselves as hosts on the BXL Refugees website. One cold Saturday morning, Pieter and his eldest daughter went to Maximilian Park and came home with two Ethiopians pretending to be Eritreans: Micky and Danny. Since they were both on their way to England, the plan was to host them for a limited amount of time.

A few days later, Micky and Danny asked Pieter and Olivia if they could host a few Ethiopian people they knew. They agreed, then more Ethiopian asylum seekers followed. The family discussed the situation and settled on a compromise to host another two refugees for two days a week. However, soon enough, things did not go according to plan. Since the Ethiopians had failed to make it to England, they stayed much longer than anticipated. There were also more of them than originally planned. By the time summer arrived, the Ethiopians were still living with Pieter and Olivia. At the height of the operation, they were hosting seven asylum seekers: Natty, Josie, Santa, Yared and Amy, in addition to Micky and Danny. They slept in the attic, but also regularly used other parts of the house and garden. So it was not always easy for the family.

The Ethiopians knew each other from the time spent together in an open refugee centre in Germany. They had been in Europe for more than three years without ever having obtained a permanent residence permit. Some of them had flown to Germany on a forged tourist visa. Once they arrived, and after the visa had expired, they applied for asylum. Others had taken one of the eastern routes by land and sea. They had very different backgrounds: those who had travelled to Europe by plane came from relatively well-off families, while those who had travelled under their own steam, like Danny, came from very poor families.

Two or three times a week, they tried to find a way to get to England at night. But each time they failed. Occasionally, they were arrested: the police would take them to a closed centre (like the one in Bruges) for a few days. Some were also transferred back to Germany because that was where they had submitted their original application (and where, according to the Dublin Regulation, the application had to be processed).

Every time their attempts to reach the United Kingdom failed, the Ethiopians got more and more desperate and depressed. Natty, the only one who spoke English, confided in Olivia. He was at his wits' end, telling her that he 'wanted to be someone again'. He also revealed that they had come not from Eritrea but from the Ethiopian capital Addis Ababa. Listening to his story, Olivia could tell that Danny came from a very poor family, unlike Micky and Natty.

The situation also became increasingly complicated for Pieter, Olivia and their children. So in the summer of 2018, they made a proposal to the group: a voluntary, funded return to Ethiopia. The group all owed their families for having fronted them the money to cover the costs of the journey. These costs amounted to between €3,000 and €11,000 per person. Pieter and Olivia proposed organising fundraising campaigns to both repay these debts and also provide them with an amount to start up a new economic activity together in Ethiopia. Micky, Danny and Natty agreed to the proposal, while the others stuck to their plan to reach the United Kingdom.

Pieter and Olivia organised several Ethiopian Nights: fundraising dinners where they invited friends and other people they knew to enjoy some delicious Ethiopian dishes prepared by the group in exchange for sponsorship. The goal was to raise €26,500. That was the amount that was needed to repay Micky, Danny and Natty's debts and to provide them with the startup capital.

Pieter scheduled meetings with the NGO Caritas International, which regularly supports voluntary return projects. But never before had they seen asylum seekers deciding to work together on a new business in their country of origin. The Caritas employees were impressed.

During the summer of 2018, Pieter contacted me to mull over a realistic business plan for a new company in Ethiopia. I saw the first, rudimentary concept to set up a travel agency in Ethiopia that would target European tourists. The plans were not very realistic. How did they think they would compete with the existing, well-organised travel sector in Ethiopia? Having previously met the passionate Bob Elsen from the Belgian travel agency Joker, who promotes sustainable tourism and had also set up successful ViaVia travel cafés in various countries, I suggested that they speak to him. So Pieter organised a meeting with Bob. Joker had just closed a ViaVia Café in Addis Ababa and was willing to consider reopening it if they could find someone who would manage it properly, and who would also provide the necessary funding. Bob appreciated the entrepreneurial spirit of Micky, Danny and Natty: taking the brave step to leave their country was evidence enough that they were not afraid of a challenge. Meanwhile, I contacted the microfinance institution Wasasa to see if they could finance the trio's business project upon their return. Pieter then travelled to Ethiopia for a few weeks and met many people, including Amasalu Alemayehu, the CEO of Wasasa Microfinance. But the trio were not really sold on the ViaVia Café plan. Pieter also increasingly realised that he was the only one working on the plan, which gradually started to annoy him.

The plan to set up a joint business activity eventually fizzled out. Instead, the Ethiopians proposed individual projects. Micky set his sights on a restaurant in Addis Ababa. Natty wanted to set up an IT and print shop. And Danny dropped out and revived his plan to make it to England.

What has become of them since 2018? Thanks to Pieter and Olivia, Micky and Natty were able to return to Ethiopia. And thanks to the fundraising activities, they were also able to repay their debts. Both received an additional sum of €5,000 to develop a new economic activity. While nothing came of Micky's restaurant, he did use the €5,000 to invest in a second-hand car and became a taxi driver. His mother had become very ill, so his return gave him the opportunity to be by her side for her final months. Pieter and Olivia have not heard anything from Natty since he went back to Ethiopia. His return was more complex because he first had to get permission from his uncle in Ethiopia. Danny finally made it to England, where Pieter and Olivia visited him in Nottingham. He is going through a recognition procedure and is doing quite well. As an asylum seeker, he receives £60 a week. Through less official channels, he earns an additional £3.50 per hour, the only way he can make ends meet. England is attractive to asylum seekers and refugees because you are not required to carry an identity card, making it easier to live under the radar there. Only Amy managed to obtain a residence permit in England. She is doing well and is also now married.

When I ask Pieter and Olivia how they look back on their initiative, I get very interesting answers. Both confirm that they certainly do not regret their approach. Pieter is quite critical of the group of Ethiopians and believes that they would have been better off never having left their country. He refers to *The Year of the Runaways* by the Indian author Sunjeev Sahota about the ups and downs of three young Indian men in northern England. Olivia sees it as less black and white and points out that for some, like Danny, his journey to Europe was not only driven by so-called pull factors (attracted by the prosperity in Europe), but that his life in poverty was so awful that he had no choice but to leave Ethiopia. For him, this was a push factor: he was forced to flee because he feared for his life, even though there was no risk of persecution.

What can I conclude from this story? It illustrates how the opportunity to work and earn an income in your own region is perhaps the best way of tempering the urge to migrate. By the same token, deterrence and more robust borders don't seem to do enough to slow down migration.

A summary of migration in Africa

Since a link is often made between the demographic time bomb in Africa and the threat of large-scale migration to Europe, I would like to briefly delve deeper into the migration issue.

In addition to the demographic factors (and the search for better working and living conditions), there are, of course, many other reasons why people migrate: drought, violence, the political situation, cultural and religious factors and so on.

In terms of *where* people migrate to, this can be to other countries within the African continent (intracontinental) or to richer, more developed countries (intercontinental).

Migration in sub-Saharan Africa is predominantly an intra-African affair. Of the 40.5 million African (international) migrants, 21 million live in another African country.[32] Violent conflicts have led to large refugee flows. Uganda, for example, hosts 1.3 million refugees from eastern Congo, South Sudan, Burundi and Rwanda.[33] And in the global top 10 of countries of origin, you will find seven countries from sub-Saharan Africa: Sudan, South Sudan, Burundi, Eritrea, Congo, Somalia and the Central African Republic,[34] all countries prey to internal conflicts. Furthermore, in the global top ten of countries with the highest number of internally displaced persons (refugees within their own borders), there are six African countries: Congo, Somalia, Nigeria, Sudan, Ethiopia and South Sudan. Sudan currently has 11.5 million internally displaced persons, the highest number worldwide.[35]

Let us now look at how intercontinental migration from Africa to Europe has evolved over the last 30 years. We can use statistics from the Population Division of the United Nations Department of Economic and Social Affairs (UNDESA), which takes 'stock' of the number of international migrants every five years.[36] Statisticians use this concept to count the number of migrants present at a specific point in time. Stock data takes a snapshot of the situation at any given moment. It is also the opposite of 'flow', which – as the name suggests – maps migration flows (in and out). Thanks to these five-yearly snapshots, we can monitor changes in the composition of the migrant population over time. The UNDESA figures are based on national data, where a migrant is defined as 'a person who was not born in the country in which he resides'.[37] These figures include people who have been granted the nationality of their country of residence and asylum seekers on the 'waiting list'. People whose parents were migrants (commonly referred to as 'second-generation migrants', although this is not an adequate term) are *not* included in the figures.

Figure 4 shows the number of migrants in Europe[38] that come from Africa. A distinction is made between sub-Saharan Africa and the Maghreb countries. About 11 million migrants from Africa live in Europe currently. Around half of these came from the Maghreb countries and the other half from sub-Saharan Africa. Together they account for approximately 2.4 per cent of the EU population.

In 2020, Europe had 87 million migrants, 43 million of whom came from outside the EU.[39] African migrants therefore make up approximately a quarter of the migrant population from outside the EU.

As mentioned, UNDESA's figures do not take into account people whose parents (or grandparents) were migrants. According to a recent OECD report, the group of native-born people with at least one foreign-born parent makes up 7.3 per cent of the EU population.[40] The OECD report does not provide any details on the geographical origin of this group. But this is something Belgium, for example, does publish statistics on: first-generation migrants from North Africa and sub-Saharan Africa, together with people whose parents (or grandparents) come from North Africa and sub-Saharan Africa, make up 8.8

FIGURE 4 Evolution of migration from sub-Saharan Africa and Maghreb to Europe (stock). Source: United Nations, DESA, International Migration Stock 2020, Destination and Origin, own graph based on 'International migrant stock at mid-year by sex and by region, country or area of destination and origin, 1990–2020' (POP/DB/MIG/Stock/Rev.2020).

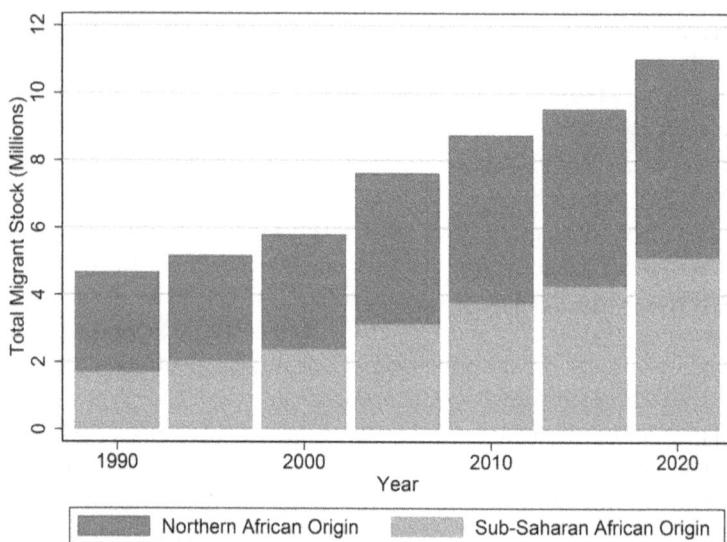

per cent of the Belgian population.[41] I contacted the EU Directorate General Eurostat to request similar figures for the entire EU and got the following response: 'Unfortunately, as you can see, we do not have data on 2nd and 3rd generation immigration.'[42] I have to assume that the EU figures would be roughly the same, perhaps slightly lower.

The conclusion is twofold. Actual primary migration from Africa to Europe remains relatively limited. But if you also include people from subsequent generations with a migration background from that region, then the group of citizens with an African migration background is significant.

Migrants or refugees

It is important to distinguish between the broad concept of migrant and the specific concept of refugee. Migrants are people who, for whatever reason, have left their country of origin. This includes both people who left voluntarily and people who left out of necessity. Refugees are people who, because of a well-founded fear of persecution for reasons of race, religion, nationality, membership in a social group or political opinion, find themselves outside their country and cannot or do not wish to seek the protection of their own country because of that fear. So refugees make up a subsection of the broad population of migrants. They also fall under the protection of the Convention Relating to the Status of Refugees (also known as the Geneva Convention or the Refugee Convention) that was adopted in 1951.

Never before has our world seen more migrants and refugees. And the recent crisis in Ukraine has done nothing to reverse this trend. According to the International Organization for Migration (IOM), the number of (international) migrants worldwide stood at 281 million in 2020.[43] But accounting for just 3.6 per cent of the global population, international migration remains – relatively speaking – limited. Furthermore, the number of refugees is 'only' 26.4 million[44] or less than 10 per cent of the migrant population.

Different visions

Oxford professors Paul Collier and Alexander Betts have carried out extensive research into migration. Their conclusions are certainly not shared by everyone, but they do provide food for thought. They indicate that the protection of refugees is an ethical 'non-reciprocal obligation'.[45] Just as it is a non-reciprocal obligation – with reference to philosopher Immanuel Kant: a categorical imperative – to save a drowning child, regardless of who that child is or where they have come from.[46] Collier and Betts distinguish refugees from 'economic migrants', who, in their view, are primarily looking for a better life. Unlike refugees, economic migrants can choose freely whether or not to migrate, according to Collier and Betts. Economic migrants as such are not eligible for protection under the Refugee Convention. Collier and Betts point out that there is no universal right to move to a country of your choice.[47] They argue that countries that receive economic migrants are neither ethically nor legally obliged (under international law) to do so. In their view, when countries receive economic migrants, they do so on the basis of reciprocal obligations, that is, common interest and mutual consent. For example, because they are facing labour market shortages and want to attract foreigners to help plug the gaps.

While the Oxford professors see fundamental limitations in the right to economic migration and to go and live in another country, Dutch researchers Henk van Houtum and Leo Lucassen prefer to talk about 'labour migration'. They believe that migration, including labour migration, is a normal part of human society.[48] They are in favour of a proactive and flexible labour migration policy that benefits both migrants and the EU. Their view is diametrically opposed to that of Collier and Betts.

It is very hard to predict how migration from Africa to Europe will evolve in the future. Stephen Smith, an Africa expert who made a great impression on French president Emmanuel Macron, defiantly claimed that if migration flows between Africa and Europe were to reach the same level as those between Mexico and the United States in the period 1975–2010, then between now and 2050, Europe might be faced with 150 million African migrants (including future generations).[49] In light of the statistics mentioned earlier, we are still a long way from those projections. Academic studies also qualify Stephen Smith's predictions as 'alarmist'. Instead, they assume a steady growth in migration from Africa to Europe.[50]

Paul Collier, the Oxford professor we just met, sees three determinants for international migration.[51] Firstly, the intensity of migration is caused by the income gap between the origin country and the destination country. The bigger the gap, the more attractive the destination country becomes. Then there is the cost of the migration itself. This is an 'investment' made by the departing migrant or their family, as we saw in the story about the Ethiopian transmigrants. The expected economic return of migration must outweigh the cost of the investment. Finally, there is the importance of the presence of a diaspora in the destination country because this leads to an easier reception there.

Like Stephen Smith, Collier is pessimistic about the impact of African demography on future migration flows. He believes we are seeing 'the beginnings of disequilibrium of epic proportions'.[52]

As mentioned, Van Houtum and Lucassen disagree with Collier. They write that research into the motives of migrants shows that, for many, migration is an exceptional decision: leaving your family, friends, familiar country and local environment for an uncertain, difficult future is a big step. In addition, the migrant must have money, contacts and a lot of perseverance because Europe is one of the most expensive places in the world. All these factors explain why the number of labour migrants from North and West Africa is relatively small.[53]

The increase in international migration is putting European society under a great deal of pressure. A pressure that is real, even though its impact is often exaggerated by politicians from far-right parties. There is no support in Europe for an 'open borders' policy.

However, the situation is more complex than it initially seems. Europe is not so much being overrun by migrants in search of a better life. It is the European economy itself that is attracting migrants to fill menial jobs. Dutch migration expert Hein De Haas puts forward a convincing argument. Shedding new light on the dynamics of migration flows, he consigns traditional narratives to the wastepaper basket. He rejects the 'push–pull' theory, which states that migrants have no choice but to migrate and are attracted by the prosperity of Europe. In doing so, he shows that the demand for labour, especially for menial workers, is the biggest driver of migration in Europe.[54] Therefore, it is Europe itself causing these international migration flows. Migrants generally do the work that non-migrants no longer want to do, usually low-status jobs that are dirty, dangerous and demeaning. Examples include domestic work, cleaning, catering, construction and transport. The number of European workers willing to do this kind of work has declined, a view that is generally held back in the political discourse.

At the same time, I remain firmly convinced that encouraging decent work in countries of origin is fundamentally important, both ethically and economically. This approach takes time and patience and therefore features less in the political debate. I have spoken to hundreds of African small business owners over the past 20 years. Not one of them has ever told me they wanted to migrate to Europe. On the contrary, they all wanted a better future for their business and a better life in their own country, in Africa. If people have decent work, the option of migrating becomes irrelevant.

Debates and publications regularly point out that improving living conditions in the countries of origin (in Africa) will lead to greater migration flows to Europe. Econometrists have found that – to a certain extent – there is a positive correlation between the rising income of a developing country and the increase in emigration.[55] As soon as a country reaches an average income per capita of $10,000, emigration then decreases again. The correlation between emigration and income (up to $10,000 income per capita) could be explained by the fact that migration is expensive. People in countries with a higher level of prosperity are therefore more likely to be able to afford to emigrate. In addition, emigration presupposes a certain degree of planning and therefore of education. So migration is more likely to occur from the somewhat more prosperous countries. Based on these findings, some have claimed that there is no point in contributing to the economic development of Africa because this would only lead to even more emigration. Recent statistical research has shown that the observed correlation is skewed by higher migration flows from middle-income countries, which are geographically closer to the destination countries and more frequently have colonial ties. 'However, in policy-relevant time periods of 5 to 10 years economic growth coincides with less emigration. Hence, policy makers should not be too concerned about trade-offs between development cooperation and immigration control. Even in very poor countries improving economic conditions rather discourage people from migrating, at least at the margin.'[56] Consequently, the fear that greater economic prosperity in Africa will lead to more migration is unfounded.

Congolese refugees in Kenya

To escape violence and persecution, many African refugees migrate to a neighbouring country within their own continent. Their situation is particularly desperate, something I saw first-hand while visiting Congolese refugees near Nairobi. I had met them through the Kenyan NGO Tushirikiane ('solidarity' in Swahili), Tusa for short.[57] This NGO helps refugees from the Great Lakes region with various forms of support: trauma processing, medical care, treatment of often malnourished children, education, language lessons (they speak neither English nor Swahili), advice on starting up economic activities, financial services and so on.

In Mihango, a poor suburb of Nairobi, I met 32 women who were part of a Tusa self-help group. They had all come from eastern Congo, having fled the violence of the armed rebel movement M23 that has brought death and destruction to the region. Most of the women had very young children. And their husbands were nowhere to be seen: they had either died or left their wives. The horror stories about what the women had experienced and about how they had been driven from their fields and homes grabbed me by the throat. They had travelled straight through neighbouring Uganda to the Kenyan capital Nairobi, as stopping in Uganda would have meant being forced to live in a refugee camp. In Kenya, refugees have relatively more freedom.

Tusa supports 32 solidarity groups and self-help groups, which together have more than 1,200 members. Including their children, these groups account for approximately 7,000 refugees. Solidarity groups mainly focus on trauma processing and social guidance. Meanwhile, the self-help groups try to start up joint economic activities so that members can earn a modest income for their families. Since the 2021 Kenyan Refugee Act, refugees in Kenya are – in principle – allowed to engage in economic activities. The group of women from Mihango had therefore recently started a small chicken farm using their own resources and with financial support from Tusa. On the day I visited, the chicks had just arrived. A Congolese veterinarian was assisting the women's group. Although it was a very rudimentary coop, the vet was extremely focused on cleanliness and hygiene. The aim of the women is to earn an independent basic income by rearing the chicks. Afterwards, I learnt that, of the first group of 548 chicks that had arrived, 542 fully grown chickens had already been sold just a few weeks later. Most of the refugees also occasionally do odd jobs as a way to survive. But their situation is very precarious. They hope to use the income from the chicken farm to pay for their children's school fees, their main priority being to provide their children with an education.

However, it is difficult to run a small business if you do not have access to basic financial services or if you do not have your own mobile phone. So far, no implementing decrees have been drawn up and approved for the Refugee Act. Until that happens, refugees are not allowed to open bank accounts or have a SIM card in their own name. All payments are therefore currently made via Tusa. Together with the NGO, I went in search of a solution and saw with my own eyes how reluctant banks were to cooperate. Yet we did manage to find a small microfinance bank that was willing to participate in a set-up that will give the self-help groups access to small loans, albeit with the necessary guarantees. The latter were generously provided by the Gillès Foundation from Belgium.

Europe's turn

The migration issue is very relevant for several reasons. Firstly, the flows of asylum seekers – including those from Africa – are a source of great suffering. Their deaths at Europe's southern and eastern borders and their undignified treatment in camps (inside or outside Europe) can never be reconciled with European values,[58] even if a large proportion of the deaths at the external borders are due to the recklessness and irresponsibility of human smugglers. An estimated 50,000 migrants and refugees died at Europe's external borders between 1992 and the end of 2024.[59]

The Refugee Convention explicitly provides for the non-refoulement principle, which declares pushbacks contrary to international law. Europe has a moral (and legal) obligation to help refugees. However, there is hard evidence that border and coast guards in EU member states are carrying out pushbacks, literally pushing asylum seekers away, back into the sea, and preventing them from setting foot on European soil.

Secondly, the issue of economic migration requires a different way of dealing with international labour mobility. Solutions can be found that do not require a life-threatening journey. Thirdly, Europe continues to invest more and more in border protection, resources that cannot then also be used to support job creation in neighbouring continents, such as Africa.

Finally, economic migrants who do manage to reach Europe, and who do not submit an asylum application or are not eligible for asylum, often go underground, their illegal presence threatening to strengthen sentiment against foreigners in our society. A better response to economic migration would help defuse that problem.

Under the leadership of Commission president Ursula von der Leyen, Europe has attempted to take control of migration policy. In 2020, the Commission launched a Pact on Migration and Asylum. It took almost four years to reach a political agreement with the European Council and the European Parliament. The new rules came into force in 2024 and will be applicable from 2026.[60] The rules consist of four pillars: improved security at the external borders (with easier options for returning illegal migrants), faster procedures for screening asylum applications, agreements between EU member states to facilitate sharing of responsibilities, and international partnerships (agreements were concluded with Egypt, Mauritania and Tunisia to curb migration). The new Pact is expected to deter migration to the EU.

Nobody migrates just for the fun of it

Asylum and migration together form a very complex topic. As I am not a specialist here, I find it difficult to make firm statements about this. There are also no ready-made solutions for the numerous problems that arise on the ground. But, at the very least, Europe is bound by the Refugee Convention and therefore cannot allow pushbacks.

I believe it is important to show respect for the people who decide to migrate, be it as refugees or because their country of origin does not offer them any prospects. The line between the two is often extremely fine. Nobody migrates just for the fun of it.

Therefore, I advocate shifting the focus from protecting the external borders and strengthening Fortress Europe to supporting and cooperating with Africa. I argue for more prospects for Africa, first and foremost by creating more decent jobs in Africa.

I notice that the Marrakesh Pact supports this kind of approach. The Pact lists 23 objectives that should lead to more orderly migration. The second objective explicitly refers to a positive policy that minimises the drivers for migration:[61] 'We commit to create conducive political, economic, social and environmental conditions for people to lead peaceful, productive and sustainable lives in their own country and to fulfil their personal aspirations, while ensuring that desperation and deteriorating environments do not compel them to seek a livelihood elsewhere through irregular migration. We further commit to ensure timely and full implementation of the 2030 Agenda for Sustainable Development.'

Remittances

Migrants send money to their families: the so-called remittances, which amounted to $689 billion in 2018[62] worldwide.

In 2023, the flow of remittances to sub-Saharan Africa amounted to $54 billion[63] or approximately 4 per cent of the African GDP. The largest recipients of remittances are Nigeria, Ghana, Kenya and Zimbabwe. According to the International Fund for Agricultural Development (IFAD), migrant workers send on average $200 to $300 home every one to two months. This represents approximately 15 per cent of what they earn. What they send can make up as much as 60 per cent of a beneficiary household's total income.[64] About 75 per cent of remittances are used for food and to cover medical expenses, school fees or the cost of housing. The remaining 25 per cent is either saved or invested in assets or activities that generate income and jobs.

But there is also a flip side. Migrants are often dynamic and increasingly well educated – the proportion of highly skilled migrants has now risen to 50 per cent[65] – so their departure can cause a brain drain in their countries of origin. According to some analysts, this in turn has a negative impact on the income of those countries,[66] cancelling out and even exceeding the amount received in remittances.

Of all regions in the world, sub-Saharan Africa remains the region with the highest remittance costs. The average cost of sending $200 to the sub-Saharan Africa region averaged 7.9 per cent in 2023. The use of more advanced technology should reduce the cost of transferring money. For example, some have pinned their hopes on blockchain technology to drastically lower transfer costs. However, an OECD report warns that the mere use of blockchain technology is unlikely to solve all the problems, and certainly not the problem of last-mile cash deliveries in rural areas.[67]

Remittances are a source of external financing for the continent. In sub-Saharan Africa, the annual amount of remittances is roughly equal to that of Official Development Assistance.[68] Remittances by the diaspora are more extensive and, above all, more stable than the volatile Foreign Direct Investments.

The diaspora can also be mobilised for investments and development in their country of origin. Some African governments issue diaspora bonds to directly tap into diaspora savings held in foreign destinations. Diaspora bonds are generally held in small denominations and typically at a lower interest rate than issuances to international investors. As an example, Nigeria raised $300 million in 2017.[69] The country aims to launch a new diaspora bond of $500 million in 2025. There are also some interesting private initiatives. Burkinabés living in the diaspora contribute to the economic growth of their country by investing in Burkinabé companies. The Paris and Ouagadougou-based company ForthInvestment is actively supporting investors and beneficiary companies in the country.[70]

Finally, remittances also contribute to improving the creditworthiness of the beneficiary countries, as they provide a stable flow of foreign exchange earnings. This allows these countries to borrow at lower rates on the international capital markets.

Climate Change

Climate change plays an important role in the prosperity pentagon as there is a link between climate, migration and poverty. Researchers expect that the negative consequences of climate disruption (land degradation, drought, etc.) will lead to additional migration flows. A World Bank study estimates that the number of expected climate migrants in sub-Saharan Africa could reach 86 million people by 2050.[71] This typically means migration flows within the African continent.

Some experts believe that the impact of climate change will trigger much larger migration flows than those predicted by the World Bank. Based on estimates from the British Meteorological Service, Gaia Vince, a British scientific author, believes that the Paris Climate Agreement target to limit global warming to 2 degrees, and preferably 1.5 degrees, cannot possibly be achieved.[72] Instead, she predicts global warming of 3 to 4 degrees by 2070. According to Vince, this situation will cause mass migration from the tropical belt to the north. This belt, which includes Central Africa, is today home to 3.5 billion people.

Industrialised countries bear the greatest responsibility for climate change because historically they have been the largest emitters of greenhouse gases. I will come back to this point in the next chapter.

One of the issues caused by climate change is land degradation. The UN defines land degradation as 'any reduction or loss in the biological or economic productive capacity of the land resource base'.[73] Land degradation is the result of human interventions and natural processes, but it is made worse by climate change. In turn, land degradation has a negative impact on the climate because it reduces the absorption capacity of CO_2 and leads to higher greenhouse gas emissions.[74] In arid areas, land degradation leads to desertification. High temperatures and low humidity also lead to drought stress in crops, which therefore lose their production capacity. Research has shown that 105 million hectares of African agricultural land (including livestock grazing land) has been affected by land degradation.[75] That is an area 34 times the size of Belgium and one that accounts for 10 per cent of African agricultural land.[76] Land degradation limits Africa's income (GDP) by 12 per cent annually and the yearly cost of land rehabilitation is estimated at 1.15 per cent of the GDP.[77] So it is vital for African agriculture to tackle this problem.

The challenge of land rehabilitation and – to put it positively – sustainable land management is actually achieving it on the ground. Sustainable land management initiatives do not work if the local communities are not actively involved. It is critical that they can make the concept their own and recognise the tangible benefits, also in financial terms. A report from the Intergovernmental Panel on Climate Change (IPCC) on land degradation points out how difficult local initiatives are. It cites an example of a sustainable land management project in the Kenyan plateau, where – due to poverty, the agricultural areas being too small and the exodus of rural youth to the city – the local population showed little interest.[78]

However, there have also been some success stories when it comes to land rehabilitation. In northern Ethiopia, the Ethiopian Ministry of Agriculture, Wollo University and ICRISAT (International Crops Research Institute for the Semi-Arid Tropics) joined forces to restore an agricultural area of 7,500 hectares.[79] The project was only a success thanks to the detailed discussions and intense collaboration with the local community. The project included the construction of a water catchment for irrigation and land improvement, the planting of new crops and changes to livestock farming. The results were encouraging: crop productivity increased significantly, as did the local community's income. Naturally, these are time-consuming projects (in this case, six years) that require intense and costly support. On top of that, a much larger scale operation is required to tackle the problem in its entirety.

The changing climate not only affects the quality of the land but also disrupts temperature patterns and rainfall. Around 95 per cent of African agricultural land has no irrigation and is dependent on natural rainfall. This is because African farmers cannot afford mechanical irrigation. A study[80] calculated the impact of lax global climate policies on the production of key crops in Ethiopia.[81] As an example, it analysed the effects of climate change on the production of coffee in Ethiopia. Coffee accounts for a third of the value of the country's exports. And 95 per cent of Ethiopian coffee is produced by small farmers. By 2030, the chance of a coffee crop failure increases by a third.

Climate change and land degradation also pose a threat to African livestock production. African territory consists of 60 per cent steppe and arid areas.[82] These are often only suitable for livestock farming. Today, 270 million Africans are involved in livestock farming. Experts assume that the loss of grassland due to drought will reduce the livestock population by 7 to 10 per cent by 2050.[83] At the same time, demographic growth and urbanisation will significantly increase the demand for milk and animal products. This situation once again presents Africa with a major challenge. The only solution agricultural experts can see is an increase in productivity, including that of dairy cattle (number of litres per cow). However, this could in turn cause additional climate problems (methane emissions, additional production of animal feed, etc.). The pressure on livestock farmers has already led to competition for pasture and to an increase in violence (for example in Darfur, Sudan).

The negative impact of climate change will cause poverty and migration to increase. Mitigating the climate impact assumes that financial resources are made available for this.

***

More prosperity for all Africans assumes more and better jobs to provide families with a stable income. In the third chapter, I will examine whether, how and where such jobs can be created. But first, in the next chapter, I will look back at the past and identify what has been hindering wealth creation in Africa.

Notes

1 The World Bank, Poverty and Inequality Platform. Accessed 31 December 2024. https://pip.worldbank.org/country-profiles/IND.
2 The World Bank, Poverty and Inequality Platform. Accessed 31 December 2024. https://pip.worldbank.org/poverty-calculator?src=IND. India had 448 million extremely poor people in 1993. This number fell to 182 million in 2021.
3 Belgian economist Jean Drèze and Indian Nobel Prize winner Amartya Sen put India's success into perspective and point to the low quality of life of large

groups of people living just above the poverty line. In their view, this phenomenon is the result of a policy that is not redistributive or inclusive enough. In: Jean Drèze and Amartya Sen, *An Uncertain Glory: India and its Contradictions* (Penguin Books, 2020).

4 World Inequality Lab, *World Inequality Report 2022*, 197. WIR2022.WID. WORLD.

5 'India Has Seen Greenhouse Gas Emissions Increase by a Staggering 335% Since 1990'. *Climate Scorecard.* Accessed 6 January 2025. https://www.climates-corecard.org/2020/12/india-has-seen-greenhouse-gas-emissions-increase-by-a-staggering-335-since-1990/.

6 World Bank Group, Data Bank World Development Indicators. Accessed 6 January 2025. https://data.worldbank.org/indicator/NY.GDP.PCAP.PP.KD?locations=ZG. Amounts measured at constant purchasing power parity figures for 2021.

7 World Bank Group, Data Bank World Development Indicators. Accessed 6 January 2025. https://data.worldbank.org/indicator/NY.GDP.PCAP.PP.CD?view=chart. Amounts at constant purchasing power parity figures for 2021.

8 Stefan Dercon, *Gambling on Development; Why Some Countries Win and Others Lose* (Hurst & Company, 2022), 74.

9 Hans Werlin, 'Ghana and South Korea: Lessons from World Bank Case Studies'. *Public Administration and Development*, Vol. 11, 1991, 245–255. Per capita income in 1957 was $490 in Ghana compared to $491 in South Korea (in 1980 dollars).

10 World Bank Group, Data Bank World Development Indicators. Accessed 6 January 2025. https://databank.worldbank.org/indicator/NY.GDP.PCAP.CD/1ff4a498/Popular-Indicators#, Figures for 2023 based on constant purchasing power parity numbers for 2021.

11 Dercon, *Gambling on Development; Why Some Countries Win and Others Lose*, 69.

12 African Development Bank, 'The Middle of the Pyramid: Dynamics of the Middle Class in Africa'. *AfDB Market Brief*, April 2021. The middle class is defined here as people with a daily consumption of between $2 and $20 (at 2005 purchasing power parity, i.e. between $3 and $30 at today's prices).

13 United Nations, Department of Economic and Social Affairs, Population Division, *World Population Prospects 2022: Summary of Results*, 5. In these UN figures, a broad geographic definition of Europe is used, extending in the East to include the Russian Federation.

14 Hans Groth and John F. May, eds, *Africa's Population: In Search of a Demographic Dividend* (Springer, 2017), 13.

15 United Nations, Department of Economic and Social Affairs, Population Division, *World Population Prospects 2022: Summary of Results*, 18.

16 Ibid., 15.

17 Median of the projection interval.

18 United Nations, Department of Economic and Social Affairs, *World Population Prospects 2022: Summary of Results*, 29.

19 Prof Stein Emil Vollset, DrPH et al., 'Fertility, Mortality, Migration, and Population Scenarios for 195 Countries and Territories from 2017 to 2100: A Forecasting Analysis for the Global Burden of Disease Study'. *The Lancet*, Vol. 396, No 10258, 2020, 1129–1306.

20 Ibid., 13.
21 United Nations, Department of Economic and Social Affairs, Population Division, 'World Population Prospects 2022, File POP/03-1: Total population (both sexes combined) by select age group, region, subregion and country, annually for 1950-2100'.
22 Ibid.
23 The working population is expected to grow from 643 million in 2022 to 1,317 million in 2050.
24 United Nations, Department of Economic and Social Affairs, Population Division, 'World Population Prospects 2022, File POP/03–1: Total population (both sexes combined) by select age group, region, subregion and country, annually for 1950-2100'.
25 United Nations, Department of Economic and Social Affairs, Population Division, *World Urbanisation Prospects: The 2018 Revision* (2019), 26. Africa in these figures includes both sub-Saharan Africa and North Africa.
26 Daniel Hoornweg and Kevin Pope, 'Population Predictions for the World's Largest Cities in the 21st Century'. *Environment and Urbanisation*, Vol. 29, No. 1, 2017, 195–216. Accessed 6 January 2025. https://doi.org/10.1177/0956247816663557.
27 Rebecca Harrington, 'These Will Be the World's 10 Biggest Cities in 2050'. *The Independent*, 14 January 2018. https://www.independent.co.uk/travel/worlds-biggest-cities-mexico-city-new-york-karachi-tokyo-lagos-kolkata-kin-shasa-dhaka-delhi-a8158426.html.
28 Professor Baudouin Michel, Conversation, 1 October 2021.
29 Groth and May, *Africa's Population: In Search of a Demographic Dividend*, 1–28.
30 United Nations, Department of Economic and Social Affairs, Population Division. Accessed 6 January 2025. https://population.un.org/dataportal/data/indicators/86/locations/947/start/1990/end/2100/table/pivotbyloca-tion?df=c88fc92b-4e69-49e5-902f-1e1569212589.
31 Groth and May, *Africa's Population: In Search of a Demographic Dividend*, 333–349.
32 International Organization for Migration, *World Migration Report* 2022 (2021), 60. International migrants include three main categories: migrant workers, asylum seekers and recognised refugees.
33 European Asylum Support Office (EASO), *EASO Asylum Report 2020* (2020), 16.
34 International Organization for Migration, *World Migration Report* 2022 (2021), 45.
35 International Organization for Migration, Displacement Tracking Matrix. Accessed 6 January 2025. https://dtm.iom.int/sudan.
36 United Nations, Department of Economic and Social Affairs, Population Division, Workbook, 'UN_MigrantStockByOriginAndDestination_2019.xlsx'.
37 There are also other sources and approaches to calculating the number of international migrants. Europe (Eurostat) defines international migration based on the foreign (current) nationality of its residents. However, Eurostat's figures also have limitations: some EU member states do not share information about the origin of their residents, making the aggregated European figures incomplete. UNDESA figures are used here because they do contain data on

the countries of origin of the migrants, even though these figures are partly based on estimates and the internal consistency of the data is not perfect.

38 In the UN statistics, the definition of 'Europe' is very broad and includes 48 countries in Western, Eastern, Southern and Northern Europe.

39 International Organization for Migration, *World Migration Report* 2022 (2021), 87.

40 OECD/European Commission, *Indicators of Immigrant Integration 2023: Settling In* (OECD Publishing, 2023), 19. https://doi.org/10.1787/1d5020a6-en.

41 The Belgian statistical office Statbel does keep statistics on second- and third-generation migrants but uses definitions that differ from those used by UNDESA. According to Statbel, on 1 January 2021, 1.4 million people with a foreign nationality were registered in a Belgian municipality. This number corresponds to 13 per cent of the total population in Belgium and includes people from within (62 per cent) and from outside the EU (38 per cent). This group of foreigners includes 122,000 North Africans and 107,000 people from sub-Saharan Africa. If you also take into account Belgians with a foreign background (second generation and foreigners who obtained Belgian nationality), Belgium has 3.8 million non-Belgians and people with a foreign background, of whom 343,000 are from sub-Saharan Africa and 681,000 from North Africa. To summarise, migrants of the first and subsequent generations with African origins (North Africa and sub-Saharan Africa) make up 8.8 per cent of the Belgian population.

42 Eurostat Helpdesk, email received 5 December 2022.

43 International Organization for Migration, *World Migration Report 2022*, 2.

44 Ibid., 4.

45 Alexander Betts and Paul Collier, 'Sustainable Migration Framework'. *European Migration Network Norway Occasional Papers* (2018), 12.

46 Alexander Betts and Paul Collier, *Refuge: Rethinking Refugee Policy in a Changing World* (Oxford University Press, 2017), 99.

47 Betts and Collier, 'Sustainable Migration Framework', 13.

48 Henk Van Houtum and Leo Lucassen, *Voorbij Fort Europa: een nieuwe visie op migratie* (Atlas Contact, 2016), 118–119 and 140–150.

49 Stephen Smith, *La ruée vers l'Europe: La jeune Afrique en route pour le Vieux Continent* (Grasset, 2018), 178.

50 Dominique Tabutin and Bruno Schoumaker, 'La démographie de l'Afrique subsaharienne au 21ème siècle: Bilan des changements de 2000 à 2020, perspectives et défis d'ici 2050'. *Démographie et Société*, Document de Travail 10 January 2020, 73.

51 Paul Collier, *Exodus: How Migration Is Changing our World* (Oxford University Press, 2013), 38.

52 Ibid., 50.

53 Henk Van Houtum and Leo Lucassen, *Voorbij Fort Europa: een nieuwe visie op migratie* (Atlas Contact, 2016), 147–148.

54 Hein De Haas, *How Migration Really Works: 22 Things You Need to Know About the Most Divisive Issue in Politics* (Penguin Books, 2024) and 'Changing the Migration Narrative: On the Power of Discourse, Propaganda and Truth Distortion'. *International Migration Institute Working Papers*, Paper 181, May 2024, 19.

55 Michael A. Clemens, 'The Emigration Life Cycle: How Development Shapes Emigration from Poor Countries'. *Centre for Global Development Working Paper 540*, August 2020.

56 David Benček and Claas Schneiderheinze, 'Higher Economic Growth in Poor Countries, Lower Migration Flows to the OECD – Revisiting the Migration Hump with Panel Data'. *Kiel Working Paper No. 2145*, June 2020, 22.

57 Tusa website. Accessed 6 January 2025. www.tusacbo.com.

58 Art I-3 of the European Constitution: 'The Union is founded on the values of respect for human dignity, freedom, democracy, equality, the rule of law and respect for human rights, including the rights of persons belonging to minorities, enshrined in Article 2 of the Treaty on European Union (TEU). As recalled by Article 2 TEU, those values are common to the Member States in a society in which pluralism, non-discrimination, tolerance, justice, solidarity and equality between women and men prevail.'

59 Van Houtum and Lucassen, *Voorbij Fort Europa: een nieuwe visie op migratie*, 93, and International Organisation for Migration, 'Missing Migrants Project'. Accessed 6 January, 2025. https://missingmigrants.iom.int/region/africa. IOM data limited to African migrants.

60 European Commission, 'Pact on Migration and Asylum'. 21 May 2024. https:// home-affairs.ec.europa.eu/policies/migration-and-asylum/pact-migration -and-asylum_en.

61 United Nations – General Assembly, 'Global Compact for Safe, Orderly and Regular Migration'. Resolution 73/195 adopted on 19 December 2018, 18.

62 International Organization for Migration, *World Migration Report 2020* (2019), 35.

63 The World Bank Group, 'Remittances Slowed in 2023, Expected to Grow Faster in 2024'. Press release 26 June 2024. Accessed 6 January 2025. https:// www.worldbank.org/en/news/press-release/2024/06/26/remittances-slowed -in-2023-expected-to-grow-faster-in-2024.

64 IFAD News and Stories, '14 Reasons Why Remittances Are Important'. Accessed 6 January 2025. https://www.ifad.org/en/w/explainers/14-reasons -why-remittances-are-important.

65 World Bank, *Moving for Prosperity: Global Migration and Labor Markets*. Policy Research Report (World Bank, 2018), 28. doi:10.1596/978-1-4648-1281-1. 'Skilled migrant' refers to migrants with a tertiary education.

66 World Bank, *Moving for Prosperity: Global Migration and Labor Markets*, 33–34.

67 Friederike Rühmann, Sai Aashirvad Konda, Paul Horrocks, and Nina Taka, 'Can Blockchain Technology Reduce the Cost of Remittances?'. *OECD Development Co-operation Working Papers, No. 73* (OECD Publishing, 2020), 10.

68 Dilip Ratha, Vandana Chandra, Eung Ju Kim, Sonia Plaza, and William Shaw, 'Leveraging Diaspora Finances for Private Capital Mobilization'. Migration and Development Brief 39 (World Bank, 2023), 41.

69 Ibid., 18.

70 *Forth Investment*. Accessed 6 January 2025. https://forthinvestment.com/en/ accueil-english-2/.

71 Kanta Kumari Rigaud, Alex de Sherbinin, Bryan Jones, Jonas Bergmann, Viviane Clement, Kayly Ober, Jacob Schewe, Susana Adamo, Brent McCusker, Silke Heuser, and Amelia Midgley, *Groundswell: Preparing for Internal Climate Migration* (The World Bank, 2018), xv.

72 Gaia Vince, *Nomad Century: How Climate Migration Will Reshape Our World* (Flatiron Books, 2022), 16.

73 ELD Initiative & UNEP, *The Economics of Land Degradation in Africa: Benefits of Action Outweigh the Costs* (UNEP, 2015), 15.

74 L. Olsson, H. Barbosa, S. Bhadwal, A. Cowie, K. Delusca, D. Flores-Renteria, K. Hermans, E. Jobbagy, W. Kurz, D. Li, D.J. Sonwa, and L. Stringer, 'Land Degradation'. *Climate Change and Land: An IPCC Special Report on Climate Change, Desertification, Land Degradation, Sustainable Land Management, Food Security, and Greenhouse Gas Fluxes in Terrestrial Ecosystems*, 2020, 347.

75 ELD Initiative & UNEP, *The Economics of Land Degradation in Africa: Benefits of Action Outweigh the Costs*, 11.

76 World Bank Group. Accessed 6 January 2025. https://data.worldbank.org/indicator/AG.LND.AGRI.K2?locations=ZG.

77 ELD Initiative & UNEP, *The Economics of Land Degradation in Africa: Benefits of Action Outweigh the Costs*, 11.

78 Olsson et al., 'Land Degradation', 390.

79 Tilahun Amede, Asmare Dejen, Tadesse Gashaw, and Getachew Yimam, 'Inspiration from Yewol for All of Us'. ICRISAT Policy Brief 14, 2019. Accessed 6 January 2025. https://archive.iwmi.org/wle/news/all-us-yewol-mountains/index.html.

80 McKinsey Global Institute, 'How Will African Farmers Adjust to Changing Patterns of Precipitation'. Case Study, May 2020.

81 This refers to the least ambitious scenario RCP 8.5 (Representative Concentration Pathway) of the IPCC, which would lead to high CO_2 concentrations.

82 P. Simpkin, L. Cramer, P. Ericksen, and P. Thornton, 'Current Situation and Plausible Future Scenarios for Livestock Management Systems Under Climate Change in Africa'. CCAFS Working Paper no. 307 - 2020 (CGIAR Research Program on Climate Change, Agriculture and Food Security (CCAFS)).

83 Ibid., 22.

CHAPTER 2

A DISRUPTED CONTINENT

In the Introduction, I described how in recent decades extreme poverty has declined all over the world, except in Africa. The sizeable income gap between Africa and the rest of the world is only getting bigger. Sub-Saharan Africa currently also ranks last on the UN Human Development Index.[1]

For 20 years, I saw how Incofin struggled more with its investments in Africa than those in Asia or Latin America. There were various reasons for this: arbitrary government action, violence (for example, the ethnic riots in Kenya and the terrorist movements in northern Nigeria and northern Kenya, the rebel movements in eastern Congo), poor governance, huge currency devaluations and so on. When it came to our African investments, something would often go wrong. We, of course, also had issues elsewhere, but a considerable amount of the difficulties and failures occurred in Africa.

What has hindered Africa's economic and political progress and facilitated its underdevelopment? I will first go over the historical factors that even today are still having a detrimental impact on Africa. I will then discuss some current explanations for the disruption of the continent.

A Troubled History

Slave trade, exploitation and mistreatment

For centuries, Africa was a slave trade colony. From the fifteenth century onwards, the Portuguese – and then the Spanish, British, French, English and Dutch in the following centuries – captured millions of Africans to work on sugar plantations in São Tomé, among others, and then later on in Central America. The sugar plantations in the Caribbean and the cotton plantations in North America were run on African slave labour and, from the New Age onwards, formed one of the most important sources of wealth creation in

Europe. This has been very well documented in Howard W. French's excellent book *Born in Blackness*.[2]

Nathan Nunn, an economics professor at Harvard University, studied the impact of the slave trade on Africa's economic development.[3] By examining historical shipping registers, he was able to map out and quantify the slave trade between 1400 and 1900. In doing so, he determined where the enslaved Africans were captured and where they were transported to. Twelve million Africans were shipped across the Atlantic Ocean. Another six million Africans were traded along the routes to the Middle East, India and North Africa. Nathan Nunn sees a correlation between the magnitude of the slave trade and the current economic weakness of the continent (especially in the origin countries of the enslaved Africans). Firstly, the slave trade prevented the formation of larger communities and encouraged ethnic fragmentation, including by pitting population groups against each other, which slowed down economic development. Secondly, the slave trade undermined the formation of African states.

As a result of the divide and rule policy of the Europeans, Africans actively participated in the capturing of enslaved people in the interior. In 1807, the British Parliament passed a law banning the slave trade. Even though this law restricted the slave trade to America, the intra-African slave trade continued. In West Africa, African kingdoms captured and enslaved people to mine gold or work on kola nut plantations.[4] This led to even more ethnic rivalry.

In addition to the slave trade, the exploitation and mistreatment of the African people during the colonial period also had disastrous consequences. The excesses during the annexation of the Congo under the leadership of the Belgian king Leopold II became widely known from 1998 onwards, thanks to the regularly cited book by Adam Hochschild, *King Leopold's Ghost: A Story of Greed, Terror and Heroism in Colonial Africa*.[5] Echoing Mark Twain's 1905 indictment of Leopold II, Hochschild claimed that the number of victims ran to 10 million. Even though that figure is unsubstantiated, it is suspected that the annexation of the Congo contributed both directly (murder, violence) and indirectly (diseases, deprivation, famine) to a sharp decline in the Congolese population, which in the period 1885–1930 was probably between 1.2 and 4.7 million inhabitants.[6] Historian Mathieu Zana Etambala, of Congolese origin, studied authentic documents to describe in great detail how the occupying forces at the time of the Congo Free State (the period under the personal rule of King Leopold II) used violence to force the population into producing rubber.[7]

Africa is not the only continent in the world where exploitation and mistreatment were commonplace. Take, for example, the way in which the

Spanish in the sixteenth century conquered the Incas in present-day Peru and the Mayans in Mexico.[8] Incidentally, I find it strange that there are not more voices in Spain subjecting their own past to critical self-examination. However, this is gradually changing with, for example, the Spanish historian Antonio Espino López, who points out to his compatriots that the *conquista* of Latin America was less of a historic milestone and more of a brutal and bloodthirsty invasion.[9]

Colonisation

The specific approach to the colonisation of Africa by the European states has compromised the prosperous development of the continent. The Berlin Conference of 1884, initiated by German Chancellor Otto von Bismarck, aimed to 'regulate the conditions most favourable to the development of trade and civilisation in certain regions of Africa, and to assure to all nations the advantages of free navigation on the two chief rivers of Africa flowing into the Atlantic Ocean [the Congo and the Niger]'.[10] In reality, this conference of 14 countries[11] led to the Scramble for Africa, during which only the political and especially economic interests of the colonisers were of any importance. As a result of the agreements reached in Berlin, today 30 per cent of all African borders are straight lines.[12] For example, the straight line between Kilimanjaro and Lake Victoria divided the nomadic Masai people between Kenya and Tanzania. The Gambia became a 10-kilometre strip on either side of the river, carved out by Britain within an area controlled by the French.

Modern Africa has therefore been divided against its will and based on the borders of the former colonisers. After the African countries gained independence, their leaders showed great pragmatism by deciding to respect these borders. This despite the Organisation for African Unity (OAU) determining in 1964 that the continent's internal borders represented a serious and lasting lack of unity. But tensions did sometimes boil over. Centrifugal forces were at work in certain countries (including Ethiopia, Nigeria, Somalia and the Congo); or new countries, like South Sudan, emerged. Dipo Faloyin writes: 'The irregular births of its nations, and the short time they've had to deal with the ramifications, underlie why so many are still fighting to overcome deep, foundational challenges. It is not because Africans are savagely ungovernable or too ignorant to lead a successful country.'[13]

Paul Vossen also points to the number, speed and complexity of changes that the colonial regimes introduced in a very short space of time, for example, in agricultural practices, the introduction of monogamy, the imposition of religion, military service and so many other areas: people were torn between their identity in an existing civilisation and with their own past and striving for an identity in another society with an unknown future, but one that would be better.[14]

During the whole colonisation process, there were plenty of twists and turns that contributed to its disastrous outcome. Had alternative paths been followed, Africa would look completely different today.

Basil Davidson demonstrates this extremely well in *The Black Man's Burden – Africa and the Curse of the Nation-State*.[15] For example, he describes how from 1850 to 1860 the British seriously considered withdrawing from their African colonies in the coastal regions of (modern-day) Ghana and Gambia because they had become too costly to manage. In 1865, the British House of Commons set up a parliamentary committee to formulate recommendations on this issue. The committee advocated a withdrawal of the British from the African colonies. When it came to the Gold Coast (present-day Ghana), the committee proposed transferring power to local African traditional authorities. For the region around Lagos (present-day Nigeria), a proposal was made to transfer power to 'literate Africans'. At that time, the English were providing the enslaved Africans they had freed at sea with accommodation in Lagos and Liberia, as well as with an education. Some of them were studying in London. This led to the gradual emergence of a local, Western-educated African elite. According to Davidson, there was little racism in the British colonial bureaucracy during that period. Higher offices, including that of governor, were regularly held by people of African origin.

The vision, however, did not last long, with armed invasions and permanent colonial rule prevailing from the 1870s onwards. The British and French applied military logic here: 'Armies marched and colonies were defined, filling up the "empty map". And with this there came by the end of the century a stifling tide of Eurocentrism.'[16]

In his book, Davidson discusses 'the road not taken'. Since the British were primarily commercially driven, they could have traded with the flourishing kingdom of the Asante (Ghana) without annexing it. In the period following 1880, the King of Asante made an offer to this effect to Queen Victoria. He was willing to grant the British a huge trade concession. But the offer was rejected. In 1901, Asante was incorporated as a 'protectorate' of the British crown: 'the whole scope for possible development into modernizing structures was stopped dead'.[17]

Africa had hundreds of other well-organised kingdoms, like the Kuba in Congo or the Rwandan kingdom. None of these kingdoms survived colonisation, even though they could have easily become autonomous trading partners. Only Ethiopia managed to remain an independent empire.

Another dramatic twist was the way in which the transfer of power to the young African states took place at the end of the 1950s and the beginning of the 1960s. Within African society, a division had emerged between traditional local authority figures, who called for their former privileges to be restored, and a new generation of Western-educated intellectual nationalists, who defended the concept of the nation state introduced by foreign countries. The new African elite accepted the European model of nation states, prompted as they were by the foreign ruler. According to these nationalists, Africans had to stop living in tribes and start living in nations. Only nation states could offer the prospect of progress. Furthermore, the nationalists saw the nation state as the only way to throw off the shackles of colonial rule.[18] With this last point of contention, however, the African nationalists were adding a demand to the agenda that the colonisers had not taken into account. The African nationalists eventually won the argument.

Once in power, and after the foreign rulers had left, the African nationalists faced a lot of insurmountable contradictions. It was their intention to establish a democratic system – based on the Western model – with distinct political parties as representatives of various social classes. But the society Africa had given rise to was not divided into easily recognisable social classes and corresponding political parties. Instead, African history had been characterised by regional and territorial rivalries, which meant that the political parties were dominated by regional and territorial interests. This quickly led to regionally based clientelism.[19] On top of that, the colonial government had always been a harsh dictatorship. What the new nation states inherited was therefore less of a democratic system and more of a dictatorship.[20]

From the 1970s onwards, it became clear that the pursuit of national unity within the nation states had been a disaster. The states were increasingly undermined by kinship networks that opened the door not only to abuse of the public interest but also to violence.[21]

My uncle and the Rwandan genocide

I was born eight months before Congo became independent on 30 June 1960. As a child, I heard a lot about the country. My father worked as a chemical engineer at Métallurgie Hoboken-Overpelt (now Umicore), which processed copper ore from the UMHK (Mining Union of Upper Katanga) in Congo. So occasionally he had to travel to Congo. He would bring home samples of green malachite, and we also had heavy UMHK copper and malachite ashtrays dotted around the house. At my grandmother's hung a huge, faded yellow map of Belgian Congo. There were two missionaries in the family: an aunt, a White Sister, who was a nurse in a hospital in Bukavu (eastern Congo); and an uncle, a White Father, who became a parish priest in Rwanda. Anyone working in a religious capacity was allowed to return to Belgium every three or four years. It was always a treat to go and await their arrival at the Expo 58 terminal of Brussels airport. Once we were back home, they told us all about their experiences. A fantastic and very funny storyteller, our uncle had us hanging on his every word. So I was fascinated by Congo and Africa. I remember one day my uncle from Rwanda telling us about the hostilities between the Hutus and Tutsis. He described how he had seen bodies floating past in the river, sometime in the early 1970s. This was probably during the massacres carried out under President Kayibanda (1962–1973).

Towards the end of his stay in Rwanda, my uncle was attached to the parish of Nyamata. During the 1994 genocide, Hutu militia carried out a horrific massacre of thousands of Tutsis in his church. He had advised the Tutsi against hiding there, as it would not be able to protect them in the event of an attack, which indeed turned out to be the case. After many attempts to defuse the situation, my uncle was rescued by Belgian paratroopers four days before the genocide. The emotional scars of this tragedy in Nyamata would stay with him for the rest of his life.

Later, I met Johan Swinnen, who was the Belgian ambassador in Kigali in 1994. It is thanks to him that my uncle was evacuated. Swinnen wrote an in-depth account of the genocide, including the evacuation of the White Fathers.[22]

I visited Nyamata in 2012 during a trip organised by the Belgian Raiffeisen Foundation. It was a chilling experience. The church where the massacre took place has been left untouched and is now the Nyamata Genocide Memorial. You can still see the victims' clothes, the blood spatters on the wall and a cellar full of skulls. One of the members of our tour group was Koen Peeters, the author of a book about the 1994 Rwandan genocide. He was able to share with us a lot of knowledge and nuance about the context of the ethnic conflict. In his view, the Belgian colonial government and the church as an institution had for decades unintentionally inflamed rather than extinguished the historical tensions in Rwandan society.

Accountability of the colonial powers

What can we say about the accountability of the European colonisers for the current situation in Africa? Let me concentrate this question on the accountability of Belgium for the situation in the former Belgian colonies of Congo, Rwanda and Burundi. It is useful here to consider the work of the Special Commission on the Colonial Past, which was set up by the Belgian Chamber of Representatives (the Belgian Parliament) on 17 July 2020 to 'investigate the independent state of Congo and Belgium's colonial past in Congo, Rwanda and Burundi, its impact and the consequences that should be given to it'.[23] In the following section, I draw on the Expert Report from this Commission, which brought together more than 100 experts and organisations at hearings. After two years, the parliamentarians in the Commission were unable to agree on a final conclusion due to a serious political difference of opinion about whether or not to issue an apology. In June 2022, the Belgian king visited Congo and gave a memorable speech in which he said that 'Although many Belgians gave the best of themselves in Congo at the time, sincerely loved the country and its inhabitants, the colonial regime as such was based on exploitation and domination. This regime depended on a relationship of inequality that was in itself unjustifiable. It was characterised by paternalism, discrimination and racism. And it gave rise to atrocities and humiliation.' The Belgian king expressed his regret but stopped short of issuing a formal apology. Nevertheless, his speech was a confession of an unjustifiable Belgian colonial policy.

Focusing on Congo, the Special Commission examined both the period of the Congo Free State (1885–1908), when King Leopold II ruled over Congo as his personal fiefdom, and that of Belgian Congo (1908–1960), when Congo was a colony under the authority of the Belgian State. The Expert Report describes how violence increased under King Leopold II's rule with the exploitation of rubber from the 1890s onwards. The administrators imposed heavy quotas on the indigenous population, which drove them ever deeper into the equatorial forest. When yield was insufficient, violent punitive expeditions took hostage women or dignitaries who were often abused and raped. The consequences of this forced labour were incalculable: abandoned villages, an end to food production and the destabilisation of families and communities. The brutal violence did not stop after 1908. Massacres are known to have occurred until 1940, when Congo was already a Belgian colony. Fundamentally, this led to the profound destruction of the political, social and religious systems that had once existed.

On the other hand, the Belgian colonial administration, certainly in the period after the Second World War, did make improvements in the areas of literacy, health care and infrastructure. The Commission did add some caveats here, though. Education for the colonised population was usually limited to primary school because it was not the intention to develop a local elite. Education was also mainly aimed at developing practical skills and work ethic. Higher levels of education were deliberately withheld for a long time to prevent the emergence of an intellectual elite. The motto was: 'Pas d'élites, pas d'ennuis' (No elites, no troubles). For a long time, health care – especially for mothers and children – was only a priority, if not exclusively, for Europeans. In terms of infrastructure, the construction of the railway link between Matadi and Kinshasa, for example, was mainly intended to promote the exploitation of natural resources rather than guarantee the mobility of the population. The Commission did not deny the individual efforts of those who had dedicated their lives to education, health care or better infrastructure (I consider my White Father uncle as one of these deserving people). But these individual efforts and the reality of the improvements in these sectors do not make up for the violence of the colonial project. They cannot be seen in isolation from the project as a whole. The tangible impact of colonisation was a violent penetration and then forced subjugation of one society by another.

The report of the Special Commission identifies three important social consequences of the attitude of the colonial government. The first concerns the lack of any real democratic experience in Burundi, Congo and Rwanda. The first municipal elections were held at the end of the 1950s but did not make up for the enormous deficit in this area. The second area concerns the education of Burundians, Congolese and Rwandans. As mentioned, education was generally limited to primary school. The third area concerns the management of the colonial administration and its consequences for the ethnicisation of societies. By establishing an indirect government based on the Tutsi elite throughout the territory of Ruanda-Urundi, Belgium contributed to the creation of a strict separation between the different ethnic groups, even though it was not the Belgians who came up with this distinction.

The Belgian political class only began to engage in a public debate on Belgium's accountability for the consequences of colonisation in the late 1990s. In 1999, Louis Michel, the then Belgian minister of foreign affairs, declared that 'former colonial powers, such as Belgium, owe a large part of their development to their former colonies'. He called for a dialogue that was no longer based on hiding the most shameful episodes of the past, but on a 'dynamic of reciprocity and mutual trust'. Louis Michel led the European Delegation at the 2011 World Conference against Racism, Racial Discrimination, Xenophobia and Related Intolerance in Durban. There, he helped push for the conference's final declaration summarising the accountability of colonialism: 'We recognize that colonialism has led to racism, racial discrimination, xenophobia and related intolerance, and that Africans and people of African descent [...] were victims of these acts and continue to be victims of their consequences. We acknowledge the suffering caused by colonialism and affirm that, wherever and whenever it occurred, it must be condemned and its reoccurrence prevented. We further regret that the effects and persistence of these structures and practices have been among the factors contributing to lasting social and economic inequalities in many parts of the world today.'

Recent economic research by Professor Emizet François Kisangani mapped out the costs and benefits of the colonisation of Congo for Belgium.[24] He showed that the economy of Belgian Congo performed quite well, especially after the Second World War and until independence in 1960. The average GDP per capita fluctuated around $3,000 (at purchasing power parity) in the 1950s. Belgian Congo was internationally praised in the 1950s as a 'model colony' and an 'investor paradise'. According to Kisangani, the country had the best physical infrastructure and health care in all of Africa. Belgian Congo was an embryonic welfare state. In the period 2010–2019 (i.e. after independence), the GDP per capita collapsed to below $1,000. Despite Belgian Congo's performance in the post-war period, Kisangani shows that the major economic beneficiaries of colonialism were mainly Belgian companies operating in Congo. They achieved twice as high a return compared to Belgian companies operating in Belgium. Historical analysis of stock market prices of these companies by academics from the University of Antwerp confirms this.[25] The Belgian state budget made a net contribution to Belgian Congo of $1.2 billion in the period 1908–1950. However, the net profit of Belgian companies in Belgian Congo (mainly the mining companies) during the same period was 15 times more. Moreover, Kisangani believes that 'the Belgian colonial state was a brutal, racist and authoritarian actor. It operated within a weak civil society, with poor political rights records and a repressive political system.' The final conclusion, in my opinion, is that Belgium, despite certain achievements in the colonial period, contributed to the fragility of its former colonies. This conclusion does not diminish the accountability of the current generation of African leaders.

Plundering of African soil

In *Why Nations Fail: The Origins of Power, Prosperity and Poverty,* MIT professor Daron Acemoglu and Harvard professor James A. Robinson, both economists who were awarded the Nobel Prize for Economics in 2024, examine the root causes of 'failed states'.[26] Their research does not focus on Africa, but does include a lot of references to African states. They use a historical approach, just like Basil Davidson, but they also consider the economic dimension. Their research provides several examples from different continents and eras.

They believe that poverty is the result of 'extractive' economic and political institutions. Extractive economic institutions aim to extract wealth from the population for the benefit of one specific population class.[27] Extractive political institutions concentrate virtually unlimited political power in the hands of a small, privileged elite.[28] This elite creates economic institutions to extract riches such as spices, sugar, silver and gold from the country and amass them for itself.[29]

In 1483, the Portuguese came into contact with the Kingdom of Congo, part of present-day Congo and Angola, located on the Atlantic Ocean. It was a tightly organised, centralist kingdom with a capital, Mbanza – about the size of Lisbon during the same period – and around 50,000 inhabitants. The Portuguese established trade relations with the Congolese to buy enslaved Africans in exchange for Western weapons, clothing and household goods for the benefit of a small elite. The Congolese hunted enslaved people from neighbouring regions and sold them to the Portuguese and the English. Both politically and economically, Portugal and Congo were thoroughly extractive. Acemoglu and Robinson see a line of Congolese rulers, one after the other perpetuating the extractive behaviour of the political and economic institutions of their predecessors. From the nineteenth century onwards, the Belgian coloniser reinforced this extractive model and plundered the country's riches. Shortly after independence, President Mobutu simply continued the line of political and economic extractive institutions. And according to Acemoglu and Robinson, the same system continues today:

> The modern Democratic Republic of Congo remains poor because its citizens still lack the economic institutions that create the basic incentives that make a society prosperous. It is not geography, culture or the ignorance of its citizens or politicians that keep the Congo poor, but its extractive institutions. These are still in place after all these centuries because political power continues to be narrowly concentrated in the hands of an elite

who have little incentive to enforce secure property rights for the people, to provide the basic public services that would improve the quality of life, or to encourage economic progress. Rather their interests are to extract income and sustain their power.[30]

Acemoglu and Robinson emphasise the importance of inclusive political institutions for creating inclusive economic institutions and in turn prosperity. Since most current African regimes adopted the extractive political and economic structures of colonialism or are themselves heirs to former indigenous institutions that became extractive through interactions with the coloniser (the example of Congo), African states are not equipped to generate prosperity.

The Causes of Disruption Today

Access to natural resources

The European colonial powers primarily justified their occupation of African territories as their contribution to 'civilisation'. For example, Cecil Rhodes (1853–1902), the man after whom Rhodesia (now Zimbabwe) was named, wrote the following: 'Just fancy those parts that are at present inhabited by the most despicable specimen of human being, what an alteration there would be in them if they were brought under Anglo-Saxon influence.'[31]

In 1923, French minister of the colonies Albert Sarraut left no doubt that, in addition to the civilising mission, another justification for colonisation was access to natural resources, when he wrote: To maintain its legitimacy, colonisation must remain the greatest fact by which a noble civilising mission, which compensates and corrects the injustices of nature, sets out to create among men and things a state of material and moral progress which multiplies the means for a universal well-being. Let me explain this and let me be clear. Above all rights is the right of the human species to live a better life on earth through a more abundant use of the material goods and moral resources that can be given to all living beings. This double abundance can only come if the races work together in solidarity and liberally exchange their natural resources and the assets of their creative genius.[32]

During the period of colonisation, the European powers appropriated not only the fruits of nature (like rubber, cotton and wood) but also the natural resources of the African continent (such as ores and fossil fuels). For example, during the Belgian colonisation of Congo, the Mining Union of Upper

Katanga (UMHK), founded by Belgium in 1906, exploited the rich ore areas in Katanga and mined copper, cobalt, tin and uranium, among other things.

Even after the colonial period, Europeans appropriated access to Africa's raw materials. Just before the independence of Congo in 1960, the Belgians moved the UMHK's registered office to Belgium so that the new Congolese state would not have a majority in the company.[33] In 1966, Congolese president Mobutu decided to nationalise mining with a view to strengthening his country economically. But even after that, the Belgians managed to exact an agreement – one that was very profitable for them – with the nationalised mining company Gécamines.[34]

To this day, Western powers employ a range of strategies to obtain cheap access to Africa's natural resources. These involve offering benefits to the governments or elites of African countries in exchange for access to the exploitation of raw materials. These benefits can take various forms, including military support and weapons, and are always lower than the value of the raw materials. These kinds of strategies require not only cooperative African elites and rulers to receive the benefits but also foreign partners.[35] This is a strategy that is employed, for example, in cobalt mining in Congo (which is home to more than half of the world's reserves). Several foreign companies have extensive access to cobalt in exchange for all kinds of benefits for the Congolese elite and rulers, facilitated by corruption and a network of offshore constructions.[36] In some cases, these foreign companies receive direct or indirect political support from their governments.

As a result of the crisis in Ukraine and the problems with gas supplies, European powers have recently resumed their search for African gas and oil among not only the traditional OPEC countries (Algeria, Nigeria, Libya) but also the new African producers like Senegal, Namibia, Mozambique and Uganda. In 2022, German chancellor Olaf Scholz made a personal visit to Senegal to negotiate the development of new offshore gas pipelines. There are no reasons to assume that Germany would use unlawful practices here. Coincidence or not, Senegal has recently become a preferred partner for German development cooperation.

Climate damage and biodiversity

From around 1950, the world economy experienced unprecedented expansion. But economic growth, predominantly in the industrialised West, has been accompanied by excessive greenhouse gas emissions (see Figure 5). Africa's

FIGURE 5 Evolution of greenhouse gas emissions by region (in billion tons of CO_2). Source: Our World in Data based on the Global Carbon Project (2022) (https://our-worldindata.org/co2-emissions#co2-emissions-by-region) – CC BY.

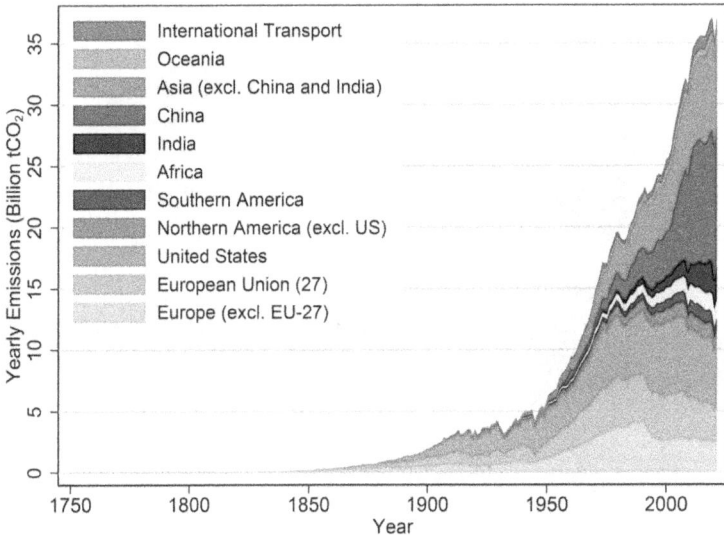

share of the global emissions is negligible, both historically and currently, with its contribution to historically cumulated CO_2 emissions at barely 3 per cent.[37] Today, Africa is responsible for 3.9 per cent of CO_2 emissions (2021 figure).

Furthermore, a comparison of greenhouse gas emissions per capita shows that Europeans and Americans emit approximately six to ten times as many greenhouse gases as Africans (see Figure 6). If Africans were to emit the same amount of greenhouse gases per capita as Europeans, global emissions would increase by almost 20 per cent.

According to the Intergovernmental Panel on Climate Change (IPCC), it is imperative to restrict cumulative anthropogenic (human-made) greenhouse gas (GHG) emissions to 3,700 gigatons if we are to limit global warming (with a 50 per cent probability) to 2 degrees Celsius.[38] It is the physical capacity of our planet, including both past and future emissions (after our planet's natural GHG capture is deducted). Of those 3,700 gigatons, 2,400 gigatons have already been emitted in the past. These emissions were mainly caused by about a billion people from the wealthy West, as a result of industrialisation and deforestation.[39] Therefore, only a budget of 1,300 gigatons for the future remains available. This means that the entire world, including about six billion

FIGURE 6 Per capita greenhouse gas emissions by region (in tons of CO_2). Source: Our World in Data based on the Global Carbon Project (2022), Gapminder (2022), Hyde (2017), Gapminder (Systema Globalis) (https://ourworldindata.org/grapher/per-capita-co2-region) – CC BY.

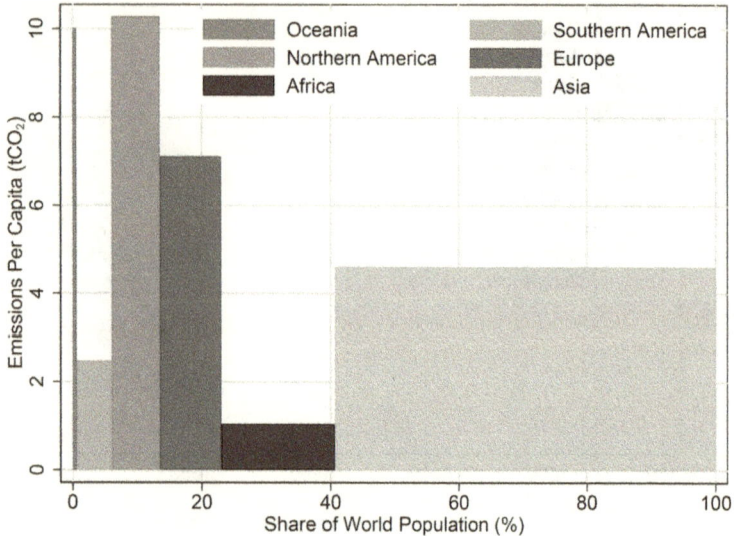

people from Asia, Africa and Latin America, has to now make do with 1,300 gigatons. These figures show how Africa, with its low GHG emissions, causes minimal damage to the climate, therefore limiting global emissions. They also illustrate that there is no longer any room for growth of the African economy using CO_2-emitting energy sources (coal, oil and gas).

The African rainforest also plays a key role in the CO_2 levels of our planet. Every year, tropical forests capture a net two gigatons of CO_2 from the atmosphere. The Congolese rainforest alone captures 0.6 gigatons of CO_2 per year, six times more than the Amazon region.[40] But it is tough for African countries to leave tropical forests intact, especially given their population growth and the need to develop more agricultural land (which we'll explore further in Chapter 3). They also contain a huge amount of stored CO_2, which would be released during deforestation.[41] The Congo Basin contains 28 per cent of the world's peatlands. Peat contains one-third of the CO_2 stored in the world's land surface, twice as much as all of the forests on our planet. The Central African Forest Initiative (CAFI), a consortium of several European countries and donor organisations, provides financial support to countries in Central Africa to actively conserve the African rainforest.[42] The CAFI also aims to conserve biodiversity, in line with the UN Post-2020 Global Biodiversity Framework.[43]

During the November 2022 COP27 conference in Sharm-El Sheikh, Egypt (also known as the African COP), African countries pushed for climate justice. Firstly, Africa and the developing countries wanted stronger commitments to climate finance by developed countries ($100 billion per year as promised since 2009). This funding is needed to support the developing countries with climate adaptation (for example, with the construction of dikes and the introduction of new agricultural techniques) or climate mitigation (reducing emissions). The climate finance commitments to the developing countries reached $90 billion in 2021.[44] Secondly, the developing countries wanted compensation (loss and damage) for the problems already caused by climate change. The principle of the Loss and Damage Fund was first recognised in 2013. But it was not until COP27 that the decision was made to develop funding for it. During the COP29 conference in Baku (Azerbaijan) in 2024, the commitment by rich countries to climate finance was tripled from $100 billion to $300 billion annually by 2035.[45] In addition, parties agreed to work together to scale up funding, from both public and private sources, to developing countries to the amount of $1.3 trillion per year by 2035. In the Nairobi Declaration at the end of the 2023 African Climate Summit in Kenya, African leaders wrote that Africa can play a key role in the fight against climate disruption, partly because the continent has 40 per cent of the world's renewable energy capacity. In the declaration, the African Union showed a great willingness to actively contribute to climate solutions, but reiterated its demand that the rest of the world make financial contributions to this, because Africa is the victim of greenhouse gases emitted elsewhere in the world.[46]

In summary, there are three climate change topics with adverse consequences for Africa. Firstly, Africa has suffered from historic climate damage and even today is still exposed to the negative impacts of climate change. Secondly, the necessary investments in Africa in terms of climate adaptation and energy transition create additional financial shortages.[47] Finally, the Paris Agreement commitments prevent Africa from developing an extensive carbon-emitting economy because western countries have already used up most of the world's carbon budget.

Even if some of Europe's current generation say they cannot be held responsible for the excesses of the colonial period of the past, the climate topic still shows that today's European generation also bears a responsibility for the impact of climate change on Africa. It is only fair that Europe contributes to this financially. The same also applies to other continents, like North America.

Failed leadership

The list of external causes that have disrupted African society to date may give the impression that the current generation of African leaders is not responsible for their continent's problems or for any shortcomings in good governance. That is certainly not the intention. Some African experts even point out the possible danger of current leaders neglecting their responsibilities because of an overly exclusive focus on the past. For example, Ernest Kakou Tigori, from the Ivory Coast, believes that emphasising the damage caused by the slave trade and colonisation in the past is more inhibiting than liberating.[48] There are undoubtedly historical reasons for the poor quality of current policies and for government corruption, but those explanations do not justify any current shortcomings.

I mentioned earlier that the European colonisers never made any serious attempts to build or leave behind democratic structures and decent systems of governance. After the transfer of power, the West also supported rulers who fit a Western geopolitical or economic agenda and who were eager to use the concept of the extractive economy to their advantage. No wonder, then, that the democratisation process in Africa is difficult and drawn-out.

The past, however burdensome, does not prevent African leaders from taking steps towards better participation and governance. What have African leaders been able to achieve on this front? What is the status of democratisation in Africa? Generally speaking, the Economist Intelligence Unit Democracy Index has been declining globally since 2015.[49] And sub-Saharan Africa is at the bottom of that ranking, with its 2021 score lower than in 2006 when the index began.

Other research institutions are more positive about the evolution of democracy in Africa. The African Mo Ibrahim Foundation, named after a British-Sudanese businessman, periodically publishes an Index of African Governance for 54 African countries (including the Maghreb countries). The index covers several dimensions: security and rule of law, participation rights and inclusion, foundations for economic opportunity, and human development. The score for Africa as a whole has improved slightly in the last decade (2012–2021).[50] Admittedly, this progress is down to the improved score for the economic opportunity and human development dimensions. The democracy-focused score for participation rights and inclusion, in fact, declined.

According to the South African Institute for Security Studies, the democratisation of African society has actually improved in the last decade, despite recent coups in Chad, Mali, Burkina Faso, Guinea, Niger, Gabon and Sudan.[51]

A number of important positive developments have taken place. Nigeria ended military rule in 1999 and transitioned to democracy. Ghana returned to democratic governance in 1992, after 30 years of one-party and military rule. In Liberia and Sierra Leone, peaceful transfers took place in 2017 thanks to pressure from civil movements. In Gambia, the ruling dictator was removed from power without any bloodshed in 2016. And in Zambia and Tanzania, civil movements have also recently contributed to democratic reforms or the avoidance of dictatorship.

For the EU, however, the recent coups in the Sahel countries are a source of great concern. From August 2020 to November 2023, seven African leaders were toppled by their own militaries (Guinea, Mali, Burkina Faso, Niger, Chad, Sudan and Gabon).[52] Firstly, Europe fears that increasing Islamic fundamentalism in Africa will be exported to Europe through migration or through its influence on the European Muslim community. Secondly, the EU is counting on the cooperation of these countries to limit migration to Europe. The increased instability in this region, deliberately fuelled by Russia, undermines this approach. These countries are also important suppliers of raw materials. At the June 2022 NATO summit in Madrid, during which Sweden and Finland were, in principle, given the green light for membership, the participating countries approved a new Strategic Concept for the next 10 years. That document considers instability in Africa to be one of the greatest risks to NATO countries, despite the fact that for months all eyes have been on the Russian aggression in Ukraine.[53]

For many years, Frenchman Serge Michailof held a leadership position in the French development cooperation agency AFD. He is an expert on the Sahel region and has also spent a lot of time in Afghanistan. In his book *Africanistan*, he compares jihadism in both regions and draws lessons from the failures in Afghanistan for the Sahel.[54] He notes that radical Islam is attractive to rural populations living in desperate conditions. The terrorist movement Boko Haram in northern Nigeria or the terrorist groups in Mali illustrate how radical Islam gained a foothold in the Sahel. Michailof is particularly critical of the usefulness of a (long-term) foreign military presence, including by UN troops. It is an illusion to think that European military interventions in Africa will solve the problem of Islamic fundamentalism. Instead, he emphasises the importance of structural solutions, including the support of strong institutions. He calls for policies aimed at job creation and rural development because these are what weaken the drivers of fundamentalism. This shows how essential employment opportunities are for Africa.

The aim of this book is to investigate how more prosperity can be achieved in Africa. Good governance plays an important role here, with good leaders generally placing importance on prosperity for their subjects. We assume that this goes hand in hand with democratisation: a democracy calls leaders to account so that they become better governors and take into account the aspirations of the population. But this way of thinking may be too European. The link between economic wealth creation and good governance is probably more complex.

Belgian professor of development economics and former chief economist for the British Department for International Development, Stefan Dercon examined how certain countries managed to bring about economic development, regardless of their past and their form of government. Dercon attributes the success of these 'winning countries' to an explicit choice by the economic and political elite for economic development to the benefit of all relevant actors and population groups (a 'development bargain'): 'Although historical foundations play a role in explaining the economy and politics today (as argued by Acemoglu and Robinson), the choices made by today's political and economic elite matter a great deal.'[55]

This kind of choice usually comes about after a country has gone through a traumatic period of suffering or violence. To be successful, everyone – including rival population groups and factions – must benefit from the choice for economic development. He refers to Ethiopia, Rwanda and Ghana, which have embarked on a path of development chosen by the elite. As a result, Ethiopia and Rwanda, and to a lesser extent Ghana, have recently experienced a long period of significant growth. Dercon notes that such dynamics do not necessarily only take place in a democratic system. He is aware of the limitations of 'gambling on development'. After years of reprieve, Ethiopia has once again been plunged into chaos. In Rwanda, development came at the expense of an unrelenting dictatorship. Only in Ghana did the choice for development coincide with a democratic transition.

Analysing the underlying development dynamics is to Dercon's credit, because these are what today determine whether a country moves towards economic growth and stability, or whether it lags behind in poverty, corruption and a self-serving ruling class. He emphasises the responsibility of today's African leaders, beyond the traumas and obstacles of the (colonial) past. In his view, successful economic development does not necessarily coincide with democratic transition.

I believe that democracy is in any case the safest path to sustainable development, because in principle this form of government gives a voice to the aspirations of the population. Other economists have shown that there is a link between democracy and economic growth. They examined the evolution of 43 African countries between 1982 and 2012 and discovered a positive correlation between the two factors.[56]

The real driving force for democratisation is the Africans who demand that their leaders serve the people and not the other way around. Every three years, the Afrobarometer conducts a large-scale opinion poll in more than thirty African countries. In its latest poll (for the period 2019–2021), the Afrobarometer found that 68 per cent of Africans would prefer democracy to any other form of government.[57] Around 80 per cent reject military and dictatorial regimes. In *Mijn leven als mushamuka (*My Life as Mushamuka), Kris Berwouts describes the rise of the youthful protest movement La Lucha in Congo.[58] This movement nicely illustrates how African civil society, especially the younger generation, is not only becoming aware of its rights but also courageously standing up for them. In Nigeria in 2020, 13 young Nigerian women (the Feminist Coalition) inspired a massive youth movement that peacefully demonstrated against police brutality by a special unit that had been set up to tackle internet crime (the so-called Special Anti-Robbery Squad or SARS).[59] The unit acted so indiscriminately and violently that it provoked a widespread reaction that almost brought down the government. A few months later and feeling the pressure from the youth movement, President Buhari decided to shut down SARS.[60] In other countries too, like Uganda and Tanzania, there are forces at work fighting for democratisation and better governance.

It is advisable to show the necessary relativism with regard to Western views on democratisation. Ghanaian UN Secretary General Kofi Annan wrote in 2000: 'Africans have much to learn from their own traditions, and something to teach others, about the true meaning and spirit of democracy.'[61] Traditionally, Africans have used mechanisms for participation through a council of elders. They are familiar with consultation processes whereby people can make their voices heard, with conflict prevention and resolution, with the importance of 'palavers' and with mechanisms for deposing inept, unjust or overly authoritarian kings.[62]

***

The disruption caused by slavery and colonialism continues to affect the proper functioning of the African continent to this day. Furthermore, Europe has willingly seen Africa as a supplier of cheap natural resources and has negatively impacted the continent with its greenhouse gas emissions. In this regard, it is about not just the historical responsibility of previous European generations, but also that of our current generation. This is crucial if we want to appeal to Europe to take up its responsibility with regards to Africa.

To efficiently combat poverty and create distributed prosperity for everyone, well-functioning institutions and driven, responsible leaders are extremely important. The legacy of dictatorial, racist and extractive colonialism has not contributed to good governance. But many current African leaders are also not going unpunished and bear great responsibility for their failed leadership. The continent must fight poverty and create prosperity despite fragile or even failing political and governing institutions. However, this is also the backdrop against which large-scale job creation will have to take place.

In the third chapter, I look at the opportunities for the African labour market in the next 30 years. Africa may not be able to count on good governance, but it certainly has an enormous amount of creativity and innovation, partly because it has the youngest population in the world.

Notes

1 UNDP, *Human Development Report 2021/2022* (UNDP, 2022), 275. https://hdr.undp.org/content/human-development-report-2021-22.

2 Howard W. French, *Born in Blackness: Africa, Africans and the Making of the Modern World, 1471 to the Second World War* (Liveright, 2021).

3 Nathan Nunn, 'The Long-term Effects of Africa's Slave Trades'. *The Quarterly Journal of Economics*, February 2008.

4 Daren Acemoglu and James A. Robinson, *Why Nations Fail: The Origins of Power, Prosperity, and Poverty* (Currency, 2012), 256–257.

5 Adam Hochschild, *King Leopold's Ghost: A Story of Greed, Terror and Heroism in Colonial Africa* (Picador Collection, 2019). Admittedly, Hochschild did hijack the 1985 book *Rood Rubber: Leopold II en zijn Kongo* (*Red Rubber: Leopold II and His Congo*) by the acclaimed Daniël Vangroenweghe.

6 Jean-Paul Sanderson, 'Van bevolkingsafname naar bevolkingsgroei: welke invloed had de kolonisatie op de Congolese demografie?' (From population decline to population growth: how did colonization affect Congolese demography?), in: Idesbald Goddeeris, Amandine Lauro, and Guy Vantemsche, eds, *Koloniaal Congo – een geschiedenis in vragen (Colonial Congo: A History in Questions)* (Polis, 2024), 107–117.

7 Mathieu Zana Etambala, *Veroverd, bezet, gekoloniseerd: Congo 1876–1914 (Conquered, occupied, colonized: Congo 1876–1914)* (Sterck & De Vreese, 2020).

8 I refer, for example, to the excellent book by John Hemming, *The Conquest of the Incas* (Pan Books, 1970).

9 Antonio Espino López, 'En España la conquista de América se ve como un hito histórico, pero en realidad fue una brutal y sangrienta invasión que debería generar vergüenza'. *BBC World Mundo*, 8 February 2022.

10 Dipo Faloyin, *Africa Is Not a Country – Breaking Stereotypes of Modern Africa* (Penguin, 2023), 42.

11 Namely Great Britain, France, Portugal, the Netherlands, Denmark, Spain, Italy, Belgium, Austria-Hungary, Russia, Sweden-Norway, the Ottoman Empire, the United States and Germany.

12 Faloyin, *Africa Is Not a Country – Breaking Stereotypes of Modern Africa*, 65.

13 Ibid., 84.

14 Paul Vossen, *Jullie rijkdom en onze beschaving: de onzin van de koloniale ruil (Your wealth and our civilization: the nonsense of colonial exchange)* (Skribis, 2021). Translated from the Dutch.

15 Basil Davidson, *The Black Man's Burden – Africa and the Curse of the Nation-State* (James Currey, 1992).

16 Ibid., 41.

17 Ibid., 71.

18 Ibid., 75.

19 Ibid., 207.

20 Ibid., 208.

21 Ibid., 227.

22 Johan Swinnen, *Rwanda, Mijn Verhaal* (Polis, 2016).

23 Belgian Parliament (Belgische Kamer van Volksvertegenwoordigers), 'Bijzondere Commissie belast met het onderzoek over Congo-Vrijstaat (1885– 1908) en het Belgisch koloniaal verleden in Congo (1908–1960), Rwanda en Burundi (1919–1962), de impact hiervan en de gevolgen die hieraan dienen gegeven te worden – Vaststelling der experten' (Special Commission in charge of research on Congo Free State (1885–1908) and the Belgian colonial past in Congo (1908–1960), Rwanda and Burundi (1919–1962), its impact and the consequences to be given to it - Appointment of experts), 7 March 2024.

24 Emizet François Kisangani, *The Belgian Congo as a Developmental State – Revisiting Colonialism'* (Routledge, 2023).

25 Frans Buelens and Stefaan Marysse, 'Returns on Investments during the Colonial Era: The Case of Congo'. Institute of Development Policy and Management, University of Antwerp, Discussion Paper 2006.07.

26 Daren Acemoglu and James A. Robinson, *Why Nations Fail: The Origins of Power, Prosperity and Poverty* (Currency, 2012).

27 Ibid., 76.

28 Ibid., 81.

29 Ibid., 299.

30 Ibid., 90.

31 A confession written in 1877 by Cecil John Rodes mentioned in *South African History Online*. Accessed 7 January 2025. https://www.sahistory.org.za/people/ cecil-john-rhodes.

32 Vossen, *Jullie rijkdom en onze beschaving: de onzin van de koloniale ruil*, 186. Translated from the Dutch.

33 Erik Bruyland, *Kobalt Blues: de ondermijning van Congo 1960–2020 (Cobalt Blues: the Undermining of the Congo 1960–2020)* (Lannoo, 2021), 138.

34 Ibid., 141.

35 Paul Vossen talks here about 'extraversion strategies'. See Vossen, *Jullie rijkdom en onze beschaving: de onzin van de koloniale ruil*, 199–201.

36 This is extensively described in the aforementioned book by Bruyland, *Kobalt Blues: de ondermijning van Congo 1960–2020.*

37 Our World in Data, based on figures from the Global Carbon Project and the Carbon Dioxide Information Analysis Center. The figures concern only CO_2 and no other greenhouse gases like methane. Accessed 7 January 2025. https:// ourworldindata.org/grapher/cumulative-co2-emissions-region.

38 Intergovernmental Panel on Climate Change, *Climate Change 2021: The Physical Science Basis – Summary for Policy Makers – Working Group I Contribution to the Sixth Assessment Report of the Intergovernmental Panel on Climate Change* (IPCC, 2021), 29. The figure drops to 2,890 gigatons if we want to limit global warming to 1.5°; one gigaton is equal to one billion tons.

39 I have adopted this reasoning from 'Special Report: Stabilising the Climate'. *The Economist*, 30 October 2021, 14.

40 Nancy Harris and David Gibbs, 'Forests Absorb Twice As Much Carbon As They Emit Each Year'. *World Resources Institute*, 21 January 2021. Accessed 7 January 2025. https://www.wri.org/insights/forests-absorb-twice-much-carbon-they-emit-each-year.

41 Bart Crezee et al., 'Mapping Peat Thickness and Carbon Stocks of the Central Congo Basin Using Field Data'. *Nature Geoscience*, Vol 15, August 2022, 639–644.

42 Central African Forest Initiative. Accessed 7 January 2025. https://www.cafi .org/. CAFI's financial support amounts to $835 million for six countries: Gabon, Congo, Republic of Congo, Equatorial Guinea, Cameroon and the Central African Republic.

43 Convention on Biological Diversity. Accessed 7 January 2025. https://www .cbd.int/conferences/post2020.

44 OECD, *Climate Finance Provided and Mobilised by Developed Countries in 2013–2021: Aggregate Trends and Opportunities for Scaling Up Adaptation and Mobilised Private Finance, Climate Finance and the USD 100 Billion Goal* (OECD Publishing, 2023). https://doi.org/10.1787/e20d2bc7-en.

45 United Nations Climate Change, 'COP29 UN Climate Conference Agrees to Triple Finance to Developing Countries, Protecting Lives and Livelihoods'. Announcement, 24 November 2024. Accessed 7 January 2025. https://unfccc .int/news/cop29-un-climate-conference-agrees-to-triple-finance-to-developing-countries-protecting-lives-and.

46 African Union, 'The African Leaders Nairobi Declaration on Climate Change and Call to Action'. 6 September 2023.

47 United Nations Framework Convention on Climate Change, *Report on Progress Towards Achieving the Goal of Mobilizing Jointly Dollar 100 Billion per Year to Address the Needs of Developing Countries in the Context of Meaningful Mitigation Actions and Transparency on Implementation* (UNFCC, 2022). https://unfccc.int/process-and -meetings/bodies/constituted-bodies/standingcommittee-on-finance-scf/pro-gress-report.

48 Vossen, *Jullie rijkdom en onze beschaving: de onzin van de koloniale ruil*, 134–135.

49 Economist Intelligence, *Democracy Index 2021: The China Challenge* (The Economist Intelligence Unit, 2022).

50 Mo Ibrahim Foundation, *2022 Ibrahim Index of African Governance – Index Report* (2022), 14. https://mo.ibrahim.foundation/iiag.

51 Ronak Gopaldas, 'Democracy in Decline in Africa? Not so Fast'. *Institute for Security Studies*, 4 November 2021. Accessed 7 January 2025. https://issafrica .org/iss-today/democracy-in-decline-in-africa-not-so-fast.

52 Comfort Ero and Murithi Mutiga, 'The Crisis of African Democracy – Coups are a Symptom – Not the Cause – of Political Dysfunction'. *Foreign Affairs*, January–February 2004, 120–134.

53 NATO, *NATO 2022 Strategic Concept* (2022). https://www.nato.int/strategic -concept/.

54 Serge Michailof, *Africanistan: Development or Jihad* (Oxford University Press, 2018).

55 Stefan Dercon, *Gambling on Development: Why Some Countries Win and Others Lose* (Hurst & Company, 2022), 31–32.

56 Takaaki Masaki and Nicolas van de Walle, 'The Impact of Democracy on Economic Growth in Sub-Saharan Africa, 1982–2012'. In *The Oxford Handbook of Africa and Economics: Volume 1: Context and Concepts*, edited by Célestin Monga and Justin Yifu Lin (Oxford Academic, 2015), 659–674. This finding is admittedly not entirely consistent with the theory of Stefan Dercon mentioned earlier.

57 Afrobarometer Network, 'Africans Want More Democracy, But Their Leaders Still Aren't Listening'. *Afrobarometer Policy Paper*, No. 85, Accra, January 2023.

58 Kris Berwouts, *Mijn leven als mushamuka: schetsen van Rwanda, Burundi en Congo (My life as a mushamuka: sketches of Rwanda, Burundi and Congo)* (Epo, 2020), 90–139.

59 Faloyin, *Africa Is Not a Country – Breaking Stereotypes of Modern Africa*, 358–370.

60 Shola Lawal, Monica Mark, and Ruth Maclean, 'Nigeria's Police Brutality Crisis: What's Happening Now'. *New York Times*, 14 November 2020.

61 Kofi Annan, 'Africa's Thirst for Democracy'. *United Nations Secretary General*, 5 December 2000. Accessed 7 January 2025. https://www.un.org/sg/en/content /sg/articles/2000-12-05/africas-thirst-democracy.

62 Vossen, *Jullie rijkdom en onze beschaving: de onzin van de koloniale ruil*, 232.

CHAPTER 3

ALLEVIATING POVERTY WITH JOBS

To get out of the spiral of poverty, people in Africa need access to jobs. Population growth over the next 30 years will also create a need for more than 20 million new jobs each year. This is a staggering number, but thanks to good entrepreneurship and a powerful workforce, the continent has a lot of strengths and opportunities to create meaningful and dignified jobs. These jobs will emerge in seemingly unexpected sectors, but first and foremost, investments need to be made in a good breeding ground.

The African Labour Market as We Approach 2050

As explained in the first chapter, the population of sub-Saharan Africa is increasing to such an extent that over the next 30 years, an average of more than 20 million new jobs per year will be needed to compensate for the growth of the working population (15–64 years old) between 2020 and 2050. It is doubtful whether African job creation will be strong enough to keep up with this population growth and avoid an increase in unemployment. It was certainly able to do so in the first decade of this century, with the continent creating an average of nine million jobs annually.[1] This phenomenal achievement was, thanks to the dynamic African economy, itself the result of the boom in the export of natural resources. But from the second decade of the twenty-first century, after the financial crisis of 2008–2009, employment growth could no longer keep up with population growth. The employment rate fell from 64 per cent in 2010 to 62 per cent in 2022.[2] Even though employment growth had continued at nine million new jobs per year, population growth had accelerated. The gap that emerged might widen in the coming decades, mainly because demographic growth might continue to exceed employment growth. A potential imbalance between the (large) supply of labour and the (relatively more limited) demand for labour will also exert downward pressure on wages.

Despite these figures, only 6 per cent of the population in sub-Saharan Africa is unemployed.[3] This relatively low figure can be explained by the fact that in Africa, informal jobs are included in the employment statistics. In other words: if you have an informal job, you're not counted as unemployed. About 78 per cent of those working are self-employed,[4] mainly in agriculture and informal family businesses. Formal, salaried jobs make up around 22 per cent of employment and are mainly in the service sector and, to a lesser extent, industry.

In 1954, Nobel Prize winner in economics W. Arthur Lewis predicted that workers in a developing economy would gradually move from the agricultural sector to industry and the service sector. Employees are generally used more productively in these sectors than in agriculture, leading to economic growth.[5] More generally, this theory says that over time, less productive sectors (in the case of Africa, agriculture and the informal sector) shed jobs in favour of more productive sectors. Since Africa's share of employment in agriculture and informal businesses is very high, these jobs may come under pressure. This is also evident from the figures. Africa's share of employment in agriculture has declined over the last 20 years in favour of the service sector, completely in line with Lewis' theory. During this period, 10 per cent of the African workforce has shifted from agriculture to the service sector. However, there has been no shift from agriculture to industry.[6]

What are the opportunities for new job creation in Africa, considering that there is a need for more than 20 million extra jobs each year?

McKinsey consultants have published three studies on the economic situation in Africa. In the second study (2016), they call for large-scale job creation in industry.[7] According to the study, a targeted policy should be able to double industrial production in Africa over a period of 10 years and create between 6 and 14 million stable jobs in industry. The consultants claim that three-quarters of these jobs can be created by Africa focusing on the production of goods that it imports and for which there is significant domestic demand (for example, in the food industry or cement production). The remaining quarter can be created by developing a competitive export industry in certain sectors (such as footwear and clothing). McKinsey points to examples of such successful initiatives in Morocco (Tangier's export zone) and Ethiopia.

McKinsey can hardly be accused of lacking ambition. But what stands out in this study is the well-known consultancy's estimation that, at best, it will take 10 years to create just 14 million new jobs in African industry, while the continent needs more than 20 million new jobs *each year* (i.e. more than 200 million in 10 years). What prospects, then, can Africa really offer to its much larger and rapidly increasing group of young people growing up in rural farming families? In its latest study (2023), McKinsey instead focuses on more jobs in the service sector, but without providing any figures.

African economist Carlos Lopes also believes that if Africa wants to create employment and prosperity, then it inevitably must develop its industrial sector. Industrialisation is a source of income and employment creation, making it absolutely essential. Currently, Africa's manufacturing industry contributes barely 13 per cent to the continent's GDP. By comparison: in Southeast Asia this figure is 31 per cent.[8]

Lopes points out that the industrialisation process that is underway in Africa is very different from the development in Latin America and Asia in the 1960s and 1970s. Back then, these regions focused heavily on import substitution: they started to produce local products for their own use, rather than importing them. Today, global trade has become a much more complex process with value chains spanning different continents. For example, a car is no longer produced in one place but is the result of a very complex logistical and industrial process in which parts are produced and assembled in various places all over the world. The import substitution model is therefore barely still applicable: it is no longer possible to simply replace the import of finished goods (e.g. agricultural machinery) with local production.

Africa can, however, tap into the huge domestic demand for food to ensure that its own food industry is able to feed the continent. Every year, the African continent buys $43 billion worth of food from the rest of the world because of the inefficiencies of its own agricultural processing industry and food production.[9] Main food imports are wheat, rice, soya beans, oilseeds and frozen meat products.[10] Four countries – Nigeria, Angola, the Democratic Republic of the Congo (DRC) and Somalia – account for most of Africa's agricultural imports. Luckily, many countries are also net exporters. Top exports are mainly tropical commodities such as cocoa, coffee, tea and cotton. The African agro-food industry has the potential to boost intracontinental trade and its exports to the rest of the world to the benefit of its own food security, employment and prosperity.

How then does Lopes think Africa should achieve industrialisation? The region has plenty of natural resources that can be put to good use, especially mineral resources that the world is highly dependent on.[11] For example, the continent is home to 70 per cent of the world's reserves of coltan, an ore from which metals (namely tantalum and niobium) are extracted to then be used in, among other things, mobile phones. Cobalt is also still an essential component of the batteries needed for the transition to electric vehicles and in turn the reduction of CO_2 emissions. Congo alone accounts for 60 per cent of the world's cobalt mining.[12]

Lopes is convinced that Africa can develop its own growth path by increasing the value of its own natural resources and agricultural production – he calls it 'commodity-based industrialisation'. An example: four African countries (Ivory Coast, Ghana, Nigeria and Cameroon) together make up 70 per cent of global cocoa production. Cocoa is mainly grown by small farmers, with between 40 and 50 million of them working in the cocoa sector worldwide.[13] The unprocessed cocoa beans grown by these small farmers are then exported to Western countries for processing. Africa can take a larger share of the value chain by processing the beans locally instead. Recently, Ivory Coast took the initiative to build two processing plants, one near the capital Abidjan and the other in the cocoa port of San Pedro.[14] With the factories being financed by China and built by Chinese companies, production is largely destined for China.

Lopes argues that Africa should use its relative lag in industrialisation in a positive way to avoid the mistakes other continents have made, for example in terms of social rights and environmental conservation. There is still a long way to go here. Industrial zones for Ethiopian export companies (mainly in the leather industry) provide jobs for a lot of people, so they are important for development, but only if the social rights of the workers are protected. The leather industry in Ethiopia employs more than 20,000 people and the companies are often of Chinese origin. But according to some reports, employment conditions there are precarious.[15] I have witnessed first-hand the undignified and unacceptable working conditions faced by women in textile factories in a tax-friendly export processing zone near the Cambodian capital Phnom Penh. Industrialisation at the expense of human dignity must be avoided at all costs.

Agriculture and the food industry

Agriculture accounts for 53 per cent of employment in sub-Saharan Africa[16] but contributes only 17 per cent to the continent's national income.[17] The fact that 53 per cent of the working population generates only 17 per cent of the income points to a productivity problem. By comparison, the output of workers in African industry is five times higher than that of farmers.[18] Between 1960 and 2010, African agricultural productivity growth was only 0.5 per cent per year, while in Asia, it increased by 5 per cent each year.[19] Furthermore, low agricultural productivity (and the associated inefficient production methods) also leads to high food prices.

Africa is the second-largest continent in the world, after Asia. But despite having an incredible amount of land that could be used for agriculture, it is a net importer of agricultural products. In addition, the nutritional quality of food in Africa is often insufficient.

African policymakers approach the continent's agricultural issues from the angle of improving food security and safety. This is understandable, given that Africa still – and even more so than before – has a problem with malnutrition. In the period 2014–2016, there were 218 million undernourished Africans, compared to 'just' 176 million in 1990–1992.[20] Furthermore, a third of African children under the age of five suffer from stunted growth due to a lack of good-quality nutrition.[21]

In the 2003 Maputo Declaration, Africa's agricultural ministers committed to spending 10 per cent of their national budgets on agriculture.[22] The Malabo Declaration followed in 2014,[23] promising a drastic transformation of African agriculture. By 2025, the Malabo Declaration aimed to double agricultural productivity, halve postharvest losses, triple intra-African trade in agricultural products, end hunger and bring about an improvement in nutritional value.[24] These commitments all indicate the importance of agriculture to policymakers in Africa.

It is worrying that, for example, the Congolese government has never spent more than 2.5 per cent of its public budget on agricultural development, even though more than 70 per cent of the population works in agriculture. In addition, 85 per cent of the Congolese agricultural budget is used to finance the salaries of the Ministry of Agriculture and participation in international conferences.[25] The remaining agricultural budget goes to large-scale projects. In 2011, the association of agricultural NGOs AgriCongo formulated a poignant statement to the following effect:[26]

Although 80 per cent of politicians in Kinshasa come from farming families, although as young people they walked barefoot for miles to fetch water, although they hoed the fields under the blazing sun, although the income generated by their parents' agricultural work allowed them to study [...] most politicians today find themselves totally cut off from their roots. For them, farming is synonymous with poverty and their vision of agriculture is that of mechanisation, the concentration of land in vast concessions, the promotion of agro-industrial technologies on the scale of large commercial companies, or even a return to plantation monocultures.

The Maputo Declaration does not state that job creation is a priority for agriculture. Furthermore, the measures necessary to improve agricultural productivity could lead to a further decline in the workforce. But the question is whether agricultural productivity can be increased without causing carnage in terms of employment and whether agriculture could even become a source of additional jobs. Added to this already sizeable challenge is the unavoidable requirement to increase production in an environmentally sustainable way. As mentioned, Nobel Prize winner in economics W. Arthur Lewis predicted that, in a developing economy, jobs would move from agriculture to industry and services.[27] This leaves Africa with a major problem.

Coffee and nuts

In southwest Uganda, Incofin provides loans to the Ankole Coffee Producers Cooperative Union (ACPCU) through the Fairtrade Access Fund.[28] ACPCU is owned by more than 9,000 small farmer cooperatives and run by John Nugawaba, a passionate manager who primarily focuses on the socio-economic progress of the members. The ACPCU management team identifies American and European coffee traders and settles on a best possible price. ACPCU then uses the Fairtrade Access Fund to pay the cooperatives for the coffee they grow, before processing and exporting it to the United States and Europe. Once the container of Ugandan coffee has been shipped into the port of Mombasa, the American and European buyers pay back the loan to the Fairtrade Access Fund. And it allows 9,000 Ugandan farming families, who only have a very small piece of land (less than 1 hectare on average), to sell their coffee on the global market at the going market rate. In addition, fair trade-certified coffee offers farmers clear advantages: firstly, they receive a price that is on average 10 per cent higher than the price of conventional coffee and, secondly, the fair trade system guarantees a price floor in the event that the global price of coffee drops below a certain minimum level. Finally, ACPCU receives a fair trade premium that can be used to benefit the collectives, like for the construction of a new warehouse or school.

Another example is two farms in central Kenya that process macadamia nuts and that also receive loans from the Fairtrade Access Fund. The two companies together employ around 1,500 people. They buy their nuts from 15,000 small farmers, then process and package them before exporting them to Europe, the United States and the Far East. The farmers supplying the nuts usually cultivate 10 to 20 trees each (some up to 50), which were originally planted to provide the much-needed shade for coffee plants to thrive. Thanks to this diversified approach, farmers get a much greater return from their small piece of agricultural land. The macadamia nut companies also provide the farmers with advice and assistance for the cultivation and care of the nut trees. For example, farmers can get a better deal when it comes to buying young plants. An adviser from the company also comes by to teach them how to best prune, fertilise and harvest the tree. A mature tree earns a farmer $100 to $150 a year. Most of the farmers also have some dairy cows that provide organic fertiliser for the trees. A creative, innovative and sustainable approach that makes a real difference to a lot of smallholder farmers.

The disadvantage of small-scale production

Let's now return to the causes of the low production level and low productivity in African agriculture.[29] The landscape is dominated by small family farms. Research in 14 African countries shows that 80 per cent of farms have less than 2 hectares of land. This makes up just 25 per cent of Africa's agricultural land.[30] African agriculture is characterised by a mix of numerous small farms and a few large-scale agricultural areas. Most small farmers grow for their own needs (subsistence crops) or to sell agricultural products (cash crops). They have a modest income, which prevents them from making investments that would lead to expansion or greater productivity. Manual farming techniques limit their ability to cultivate larger plots of land. As a result, they find themselves trapped.

The limited scale of African farming can also be explained by the fact that agricultural land is divided (in equal shares) among the (usually male) heirs during the transition from the older to the younger generation, resulting in a constant reduction in the area per farmer. Since African countries have no or hardly any pension system, the heads of the family postpone the transfer to the next generation in order to keep hold of their land for as long as possible. As a result, it takes a very long time for agricultural land to be transferred to the younger, more dynamic and more productive generation. If African farmers could count on a pension, the intergenerational transfer of agricultural land could happen much faster. However, the pension prospects for small-scale farmers are still limited, even though the pension sector in Africa is on the rise. In 2020, African pension funds managed a total of $380 billion in assets,[31] almost 50 per cent more than three years earlier. In Nigeria, pension funds grew ninefold in 20 years, thanks to the introduction of a mandatory pension scheme. Countries with significant pension funds include South Africa,

Botswana and Namibia. So far, pension funds have only been intended for people with a formal job.[32] As a result, people in the informal sector, such as small-scale farmers, cannot benefit from them. Some microfinance institutions in other parts of the world offer the start of a solution to this. For example, the Cambodian microfinance bank AMK offers a product for customers who put aside a small amount each month for their pension ('Happy Old Age Account'). This is a modest way to encourage people to build up a pension. Of course, this is not a government-funded or subsidised pension. State finances are still too fragile for that.

My former colleague at Incofin, Kevin Kamemba, comes from a rural area in western Kenya. He grew up in a simple farming family. At school, Kevin was recognised as an exceptional student. Thanks to a scholarship arranged by the school board for him to pursue higher education, he was able to study economics at the University of Nairobi. Kevin is a real maths whizz. When he graduated, he went to work at a major Kenyan investment company before joining Incofin, where he was regional director for Africa for several years.

Kevin and I had many fascinating conversations, including those about the problems of farmers in the countryside. Kevin's great-grandfather, who had 2 wives and 4 sons, owned 15 acres (6 hectares) of land in Nyamira in western Kenya. Kevin's grandfather had 3 wives and 12 sons. Each time the land was handed down, it was divided among all the sons. This meant that Kevin's father inherited an eighth of an acre (0.4 hectares), so small that it wasn't worth dividing it between Kevin and his brother. Kevin's father therefore decided to move, buy land elsewhere and build a house for the family.

Kevin also told me that in many Kenyan families, traditions have changed: land is no longer distributed just among the sons, but daughters also get their rightful share. This is of course fairer, but it also only adds to the problem of owning too little land.

Poor soil quality and a lack of a framework

Quality of the agricultural land also plays a role. The soil in sub-Saharan Africa – contrary to what Europeans generally think – is weathered and not very fertile.[33] The soils have been impoverished by rain, oxidation and heat. These climate and soil limitations mean that yield levels in sub-Saharan Africa remain modest. For example, the average grain yield per hectare in Western Europe is almost twice as high as in Africa.[34]

In reality, a lot of farming families supplement their agricultural income with other economic activities: for example, by setting up a small business or working an additional part-time job.

European exports of cheap agricultural and food products to Africa are not exactly helping the continent get its own efficient agricultural economy off the ground. Let's take the dairy sector as an example. In 2015, Europe abolished the milk quotas that had been providing dairy farmers with a price guarantee. This caused the price of milk in Europe to fall. European dairy companies then looked for new markets outside Europe to increase their sales volumes, even at lower margins. Milk and milk powder are not directly subsidised in Europe. But there are indirect support systems that allow European farmers and dairy companies to produce at a cost that African farmers simply cannot compete with. The French agricultural research centre CIRAD investigated the impact of this evolution on the milk value chain in West Africa.[35] Since European milk quotas were scrapped, West Africa has imported four times more milk powder (actually a mixture of milk powder and vegetable fats). Depending on the region, European milk powder accounts for between 40 and 90 per cent of the market. According to CIRAD, this has had both positive and negative consequences. On the upside, increased imports enabled the continent to meet a significantly increasing demand. In addition, a local processing industry emerged that uses milk powder as a raw material. But on the downside, the milk production capacity of small local dairy farms stagnated. The growth potential of the 20,000 small West African producers had been crippled.

The lack of publicly supported agricultural research is another sticking point. In contrast to Africa, Asia invested heavily in improving agricultural techniques in the 1960s and 1970s, with the continent implementing a spectacular Green Revolution. Africa missed out on this transition, not only because of a failed policy, but also because it is geophysically very diverse and less suited to a one-size-fits-all approach. For example, the fertilisation process in Africa is more complex than in other places because the soil retains the active substances for much less time and because – due to the warm climate – chemical processes in the soil occur faster than in the north. Getting the timing right for fertilisation is crucial, which makes fertilisation campaigns more difficult in Africa than elsewhere.

Solutions and pitfalls

How can agricultural production grow without jobs being lost in that sector? An obvious solution is to increase the agricultural area per farmer in Africa. Farmers who can cultivate 1 or 2 hectares can also cultivate 5 to 10 hectares with a certain degree of mechanisation. An expansion of the area is certainly physically possible in a number of countries, for example in the savannah areas of Guinea.[36] One study noted that the average area of farms in Ghana,

Tanzania, Zambia and Mozambique (with abundant available land) increased significantly (by 24 to 70 per cent) for the period 2002–2013. This can be explained by extensification: the use of new, previously undeveloped land.[37] The new agricultural land did, however, mainly benefit the larger companies, leading to even more inequality in land ownership. Furthermore, the use of additional agricultural land in forested areas may conflict with climate objectives regarding the conservation of CO_2-absorbing forests.

The same study found that in other countries, such as Malawi and Kenya, the area of farms did not increase because land availability there was more limited.

The issue of land ownership is a very important and politically sensitive issue, because it is about legal certainty but also about justice. Good legislation and governance of property registration, which establish clear and unambiguous arrangements for land ownership, are crucial. In addition, there is a need for more fairness in the distribution of agricultural land. In 2009, the African Union issued a Declaration on Land Issues and Challenges in Africa, recommending that member states 'prioritise, initiate and lead land policy development and implementation processes in their countries'.[38] Today, many African countries are implementing a second, if not third wave of land reform.[39] As an example, Malawi has gone through three waves of land reform since 2005. However, these reforms have faced resistance, as balancing the interests of various stakeholders (e.g. smallholders vs. landowners) has turned out to be complex.[40]

It is also important that the much-needed increase in agricultural and food production takes place in a sustainable manner without a negative impact on the environment and soil quality. This is exactly what the Center for International Forestry Research and World Agroforestry and the research institution CGIAR aim to achieve: they joined forces to increase the productivity of millions of family farmers and help them use environmentally friendly techniques, especially in the field of soil management.[41] Belgian professor Rony Swennen, head of the Laboratory of Tropical Crop Improvement at KU Leuven university, has been researching bananas for more than forty years. By selecting the right bananas, productivity can be increased.[42] He believes that small farmers are currently only reaching 9 per cent of their plantations' potential, and that production can be drastically increased. One of his activities involves carrying out tests in Uganda, where he works with small banana farmers and supports biodiversity.

Paul Vossen points out that traditional African family farming techniques may be more suitable than modern, intensive monoculture with a high planting density and improved fertilisation techniques. He investigated how family farmers from the Sahel use mixed cultivation with a distance between plants (for example, millet or sorghum) that is greater than in Western Europe. Farmers sow beans in between because these crops increase the required nitrogen levels in the soil. This allows both crops to mature, even during an unfavourable rainy season. On the other hand, crops that are overly cultivated and planted too close together increase the need for water and the susceptibility to diseases. During an unfavourable rainy season, there is a greater risk of no yield at all. The farmers therefore make the trade-off between high returns during favourable years but with the risk of total crop failures in the intervening years and a guaranteed but less profitable harvest almost every year.[43]

Research highlights the importance of proper education and agricultural training. Well-trained farmers are more effective. They have a greater understanding of seeds and fertilisation and respond better to changing markets and natural conditions.[44] Decent and local agricultural training is needed, and not just for men. A survey in six African countries revealed that women make up 40 per cent of the agricultural workforce.[45] They usually work on their husband's farm but sometimes also run the farm themselves. Research carried out in 2013 found that 22 per cent of farms in six African countries were led by women.[46] However, women are at a serious disadvantage. Although they do a significant share of the work on the land, they have little access to agricultural training.[47] They are also often discriminated against when it comes to land ownership.[48]

The supporting infrastructure also plays a major role in agricultural policy, for example, in terms of suitable storage locations and road infrastructure (for transport right up to the farm gate).

Good access to financing is part of the 'soft' supporting infrastructure. In the 1970s and 1980s, many countries established public agricultural banks. They provided loans at subsidised interest rates. But it was the large agricultural companies that were best equipped to lobby for and secure most of the cheap financing. The public banks therefore failed in their mission to support small farmers.[49]

Easy access to financing for small farmers

It is important that small farmers have easy access to credit, to finance inputs (such as seeds), pre-finance harvests or buy agricultural equipment. Private rural financial institutions play a key role here. It makes more sense for governments to support these institutions, for example through a guarantee fund, than to set up public agricultural banks themselves.

In 2007, Incofin launched the Rural Impulse Fund to help small farmers gain access to financing. The fund received the support of the International Finance Corporation (IFC, the investment subsidiary of the World Bank) and the European Investment Bank. It was a remarkable initiative that provided a counterweight to the cumbersome public agricultural banks that had failed to provide small farmers with the financing they needed. This was a period when private financial institutions, which generally operated in an urban environment, started providing credit to small farmers in rural areas. The Rural Impulse Fund invested in rural, commercially viable financial institutions in Africa, Asia and Latin America, and was a real success. It also proved that small private financial institutions were more effective than large public banks.

Incofin launched its follow-up Rural Impulse Fund II (RIF II) in 2010. With a total size of $150 million, it was four times larger than the first. The objectives of RIF II were largely the same as those of the original fund. At the height of its 10-year existence, RIF II was investing in 36 financial institutions, which together provided credit to 6.2 million small farmers.[50]

The danger of large-scale production

African policymakers are sometimes tempted to promote large-scale, high-tech agriculture because it can lead to rapid and significant increases in production. Lurking around the corner here is the risk of land grabbing, with large investors buying up huge agricultural areas for next to nothing in order to cultivate them in a high-tech, highly automated way. The African Union, together with the United Nations, has even been compelled to issue guidelines for large-scale agriculture,[51] including a respect for human rights and the environment.

An example of this kind of large-scale, politically driven agricultural project is Bukanga Lonzo in Congo, 250 kilometres from Kinshasa. The project was a public-private partnership with a South African company. The project company bought an area of 800 km^2, spread over six villages with approximately 5,000 inhabitants. The project aimed to grow corn and other crops on an industrial scale. A top official from the Congolese Ministry of Agriculture told me in 2019 that he had advised against the project because the soil in that region was not suitable for the intended crops. But the government ignored the advice, and the project was a complete failure. The Congolese state lost $205 million, and some of that money was also embezzled.[52]

The rising demand for food will put a lot of pressure on additional use of fallow land, encouraging production scaling and productivity growth. A report from the UN's Food and Agricultural Organization (FAO) shows that by 2050, our planet will need to produce 60 per cent more food worldwide compared to during the period 2005–2007 to keep pace with population growth.[53] There are fears that this process will not be sustainable. Agriculture consumes a lot of water unless more economical techniques are introduced. The use of more land will threaten biodiversity and perhaps even destroy African rainforests. In addition, climate change will have a negative impact on agricultural production.[54] More positively, the increasing global demand for food, especially in Africa as a result of population growth, means that farmers, and especially family businesses, have opportunities to sell more sustainably produced food at better prices.

Sustainable family farming is key

Will small-scale family farming lose out to large agricultural companies? According to the FAO, family farming is key to the necessary growth of global food production.[55] Big companies can be more efficient, but there is still room for productivity increases in family farming. In addition, small farmers are better able to cultivate difficult terrains. As a result, they can sometimes contribute more to the necessary expansion of the area. I have often seen small farmers cultivating land on steep slopes or in areas that are difficult to access. Large farms are only equipped to work on flat, easily accessible terrains.

In contrast to large-scale farms focused on monoculture, family farmers are a more suitable partner for sustainable agriculture and soil management. Small farmers are also key to the success of soil rehabilitation or reforestation projects. For example, family farmers play a major role in the creation of the Great Green Wall: a large-scale initiative to plant a green zone in 11 countries of the Sahel, south of the Sahara, from Dakar to Djibouti, to tackle desertification.[56] The strip will be 7,600 kilometres long and 15 kilometres wide. After some teething problems, the project gained momentum from 2021 when France and the EU pledged a significant contribution (of €700 million and €600 million per year respectively in the period 2021–2025). By 2030, the project aims to rehabilitate 100 million hectares of land and create 10 million jobs in sustainable agricultural chains in the area concerned. The financial contributions to the Great Green Wall are meaningful and responsible, both from a technical climate point of view and in terms of climate justice. The project should also have a positive impact on the lives of millions of people living in the Sahel zone.

In summary: agriculture, especially small-scale family farming, is a pillar of African society and a huge provider of employment, income and food for people at the bottom of the socio-economic pyramid. It can act as a buffer to meet the need for jobs caused by the demographic explosion, especially considering the rising global demand for food. The integration of sustainable agriculture into a wider chain of agricultural and food businesses is probably the quickest route to more jobs for the continent.

The informal economy

As mentioned, self-employed people account for more than three-quarters of employment in sub-Saharan Africa. A lot of these people are running informal household enterprises or micro-enterprises. I will now take a closer look at these informal non-agricultural household and micro-enterprises, which make up approximately a quarter of self-employment. I will use various terms to refer to them: informal enterprises, household enterprises or micro-enterprises. Smallholder farmers are also part of the informal economy, but we have covered these in the previous section.

What do we mean exactly by the informal economy? When development economists talk about the importance of informal businesses, they do not mean that they are in favour of a black market or that they encourage informal businesses to evade taxes. The concept of the informal economy primarily refers to small, non-formalised economic activities that are very easy to get started with and that provide employment to lots of people. Informal businesses are generally not subject to taxes, but sometimes they have to pay flat-rate taxes. It is clear that African countries would benefit from having as many formalised companies as possible, so that the tax base is as broad as possible and taxes are collected effectively. Ideally, informal businesses grow over time into formal, tax-paying businesses. In the meantime, informal businesses are a source of employment and income for people at the bottom of the socio-economic pyramid.

Despite the prospects for employment in the formal economy, both in the industry and the service sector, it seems likely that informal enterprises will remain a cornerstone of the African economy for a long time to come. These are usually sole proprietorships, sometimes with family members working for them.

Most informal enterprises are in the trade sector. For example, all the many stalls that sell vegetables, fruit, food and clothing at African markets. There are also informal wood and metal workers who display their finished products, like sofas, beds or metal gates, by the side of the road. Younger micro-entrepreneurs sell laptops or mobile phones. Many of them combine this with selling top-up cards, or they act as agents for digital payment systems like M-Pesa. These enterprises are a necessary source of self-generated employment in an environment where salaried jobs are lacking.

According to the World Bank, micro-enterprises in West Africa make an average monthly net profit of $70 to $107.[57] However, they do not pay a salary to the entrepreneur/owner, who instead has to make do with this modest net profit. During my conversations with micro-entrepreneurs, I have often noticed that they have significant profit margins. Gross margins of 50 per cent and more are common, which is very high compared to the margins of European SMEs, but of course these are margins on very small amounts.

Micro-entrepreneurs are hard workers, with half of them clocking up more than fifty hours a week.[58] Sometimes they also manage two companies or combine a paid job with a micro enterprise.

African governments believe there is little honour in supporting the informal sector, which they sometimes consider inferior. Like all politicians anywhere in the world, they prefer to announce large-scale business investments or infrastructure projects. However, informal enterprises are essential to closing the unemployment gap. The World Bank encourages African policymakers to embrace the informal sector under the maxim: 'The informal will be normal.'[59]

Béatrice, tailor in Kigali

During a trip to Rwanda organised by the Belgian Raiffeisen Foundation, I met Béatrice Muhawenima. She runs a sewing workshop in the capital Kigali. Béatrice started her small business with just $300 of savings and was then able to apply for a microcredit of $370. She used this to buy clothes in Uganda, which she then sold in Rwanda. Over time, she realised that she could just as easily make those clothes herself, so she started buying fabrics and making clothes and other textile products. Her workshop grew into a thriving small business. Today, she employs 12 people and provides a decent income for her family of 5 children. She also travels to Dubai and China to buy her fabrics. Two of her sons and her daughter have now become part of the family business.

Breeding ground for technology and digitalisation

Africa is a breeding ground for creative technology companies that provide new, high-quality employment. The continent also has some highly advanced digital payment systems and fintech companies. The best-known example is M-Pesa,[60] which was founded in 2007 by the Kenyan telecoms operator Safaricom and the British Vodafone. M-Pesa allows customers to convert cash into digital money and vice versa using their mobile phone. This works thanks to M-Pesa's very widespread network of agents who are usually also shopkeepers or stallholders. You can find them everywhere on the streets of African towns and villages. M-Pesa enables you to make payments to other mobile phones and bank accounts. The company has revolutionised Kenyan and African payments, reaching three-quarters of the Kenyan population in 10 years. Many new users previously did not have access to the financial system.[61] This therefore represented an enormous efficiency gain. Since its launch, M-Pesa has become Africa's leading payment system with 51 million users in Kenya, Congo, Tanzania, Lesotho, Egypt, Ghana and Mozambique. The system has 430,000 agents and is therefore also a leading job provider.[62]

Other fintech companies have also emerged, offering a wide range of different services. Wholesalers of agricultural products pay farmers in Kenya digitally. Farmers can then use the credits received to buy their inputs (seeds, fertilisers) more easily and cheaply. Other examples are digital payments for the use of small solar panels (on a pay-as-you-go basis) and for milk collected by dairy companies.

There is also a dark side to the impact of these fintech companies. In Kenya, some of them provide so-called nano loans (very small loans of less than $10). These are often used for impulse buys (for example, by young people on a night out on the weekend) and then lead to repayment problems because the interest rates are irresponsibly high. Those who cannot repay the loan end up on a central bank blacklist. As a result, they can no longer take out loans from credit institutions to finance their economic activities, which sometimes leads to real drama.

The young African population is well versed in IT and all things digital. An increasing number of good-quality IT training courses are available to them, especially young people living in the cities. The quality of internet connections has also improved, thanks to the recent installation of submarine fibre-optic cables across the continent. An explosive growth of new IT companies (with app developers and IT outsourcing, etc.) is underway, with some companies also offering their services to European companies that are struggling with a lack of IT specialists. Call centres aimed at Europe are springing up all over the continent as well. The five African countries thriving under this digital transformation are known as the KINGS: Kenya, Ivory Coast, Nigeria, Ghana and South Africa.

A new Silicon Valley in Ghana and Rwanda

Bangalore is the Silicon Valley of India, having become the largest breeding ground for IT companies worldwide in recent decades. From this Indian city, these companies provide remote IT support to organisations all over the world. In addition, countless major foreign companies have chosen Bangalore to set up IT departments to manage their global IT operations. There are reportedly 1.5 million IT specialists working in Bangalore, three times as many as in the American Silicon Valley. Providing a real boost for Bangalore, this transformation can be credited to excellent IT training and a high number of young IT graduates.

Africa also has a growing number of well-educated, young and very smart IT engineers. Recently founded, the Next Einstein Forum's mission is as follows: 'Our work is shaped by our belief that the next Einstein will be African. We are working to make Africa a global hub for science and technology.'[63] The initiative is supported by companies like Johnson & Johnson and the Mastercard Foundation. They strongly believe in the huge intellectual potential of the young African population. Perhaps African IT companies will eventually become strong competitors to their Indian counterparts.

The passionate German entrepreneur Martin Hecker is firmly convinced of the job potential of the African IT sector and also has the evidence to prove it. I met him at an economics and development conference in Cologne where he was presenting the company Amalitech.[64] His company provides young African IT engineers in Ghana and Rwanda with additional training (after their bachelor's or master's degree in IT) and then recruits them to provide remote IT services to German companies. The employees all receive a permanent contract. Amalitech was only founded in 2019, but by 2025 it will have already trained 3,000 IT engineers and have 1,000 employees. The training courses are co-financed by the German Ministry of Development Cooperation with Amalitech's customers being medium-sized German companies. Amalitech is a social enterprise that first and foremost aims to create as many high-quality jobs as possible in Africa. Martin Hecker founded the company after a career of more than twenty years at Boston Consulting Group.

When he left, he wanted to put his talents and energy to full use to help Africa. Despite its social mission, the company is already breaking even.

Martin Hecker believes that the African IT ecosystem has a number of advantages compared to India. And it is quite a compelling list. First of all, there is the high-quality hard and soft infrastructure in the countries where Amalitech works (Ghana, Rwanda). Not only are there excellent fibre-optic connections, but Africa also has the advantage of being in the same time zone as Europe. The employees speak good, understandable English. The second factor is cultural. Amalitech has a very informal, non-hierarchical culture that allows teamwork to thrive. Mistakes are talked about openly, which means that there is no loss of face or fear of admitting that there is an issue. On the contrary, mistakes are seen as an opportunity to address problems and make improvements. I experienced the same culture on the governing board of an African institution, where signals of mutual trust and respect were exchanged, meaning that people were not afraid of their hierarchical superiors and could admit to mistakes without losing face or recriminations. This was made possible thanks to a particular kind of fraternity that I had rarely experienced before. The final reason for Amalitech's success is that the company does not suffer from high employee turnover. German medium-sized companies that cannot afford to set up their own IT department are looking for an IT partner with a stable team of staff. Amalitech employees are not job hoppers.

Martin Hecker is confident that his company, together with others in this sector, will create approximately ten thousand jobs for IT professionals in Ghana and Rwanda by 2030. He believes that this will represent a breakthrough in the rise of IT companies in Africa, providing a significant boost to employment. In addition to Ghana and Rwanda, he also sees other countries in Africa with similar potential, including Kenya, Nigeria, South Africa, Senegal and Uganda.

I also find this an interesting model because it allows people in these countries to work for European companies without having to embark on a dangerous migration journey of thousands of kilometres.

The blue economy

There are 38 African countries with direct access to the ocean, and the continent also boasts some huge lakes, like Lake Victoria or Lake Tanganyika. This offers maritime and water-related opportunities, the so-called blue economy, which today employs almost 50 million Africans. 'If fully exploited and well managed, Africa's Blue Economy can constitute a major source of wealth and catapult the continent's fortunes', writes the United Nations Commission for Africa in its policy handbook for the African Blue Economy.[65] Some African countries are very dependent on the blue economy. This is the case for Cape Verde, Comoros, Kenya, Madagascar, Mauritius, Mozambique, Seychelles and South Africa.[66]

The African Union has developed a strategy to increase employment in the blue economy by 60 per cent in the very long term (40 years).[67] The strategy focuses on 10 different sectors: ports, transport, aquaculture, blue energy (e.g. offshore wind projects), minerals (deep sea mining), oil and gas, coastal tourism, blue carbon and ecosystems (carbon sequestration through wetlands and mangroves), research and education. From a financial-economic point of view, coastal tourism, oil and gas, and minerals are the most important sectors. However, when comparing the employment provision of the different sectors, coastal tourism and fishery are the most prominent. This is what we will now discuss further.

Coastal tourism employs 24 million people. The potential of this sector is enormous. The African Union estimates that employment in the sector can increase by another 50 per cent. Admittedly, the negative environmental impact of coastal tourism can be quite large (loss of biodiversity, pollution by hotels and cruise ships, etc.). That is why the African Union is pushing for the development of ecotourism to protect ecosystems and limit the ecological footprint. The Kenyan government, among others, supports this approach.

The fishing industry, both coastal and inland, employs 13 million people. In addition, fish is an important source of animal protein and has a high nutritional value. However, the African fishing industry is very underdeveloped. The low level of technology means that fishing is not very productive. In various African countries, I have seen first-hand what life is like for fishermen at sea (Guinea, Senegal, Tanzania) or inland (Congo River, Lake Victoria, Lake Albert). They work in very precarious and risky conditions. Furthermore, the cold chain from fishing to selling is in many cases very poorly developed. Aquaculture is on the rise (e.g. in Nigeria and Egypt) and can make the sector more efficient.

But fisheries are threatened by overfishing. In addition, illegal fishing by fishermen from outside the African continent is rampant. Coastal areas are exposed to erosion, loss of biodiversity and pollution (Africa is estimated to be the second-biggest ocean plastic polluter). These phenomena are exacerbated by climate change, which leads to rising sea levels, heat waves, tidal waves and storms. In turn, heat waves lead to significant reductions in fish.[68]

Rising sea levels pose a threat to the Small Island Development States (like the Seychelles). There is an urgent need for integrated coastal management: developing sustainable blue infrastructure, adequately managing natural habitats and natural resources, and addressing pollution, which is threatening the productivity of Africa's coastal and marine ecosystems. If managed well, the marine and coastal ecosystems will provide the continent's coastal countries and communities with food, a livelihood and economic opportunities while protecting them against the ravages of climate change.

An interesting example of an innovative financial instrument supporting coastal management is the Seychelles Blue Bond.[69] The Seychelles launched the world's first sovereign blue bond and raised $15 million. It is a pioneering financial instrument designed to support sustainable marine and fisheries projects. The bond will include support for the expansion of marine protected areas, improved governance of priority fisheries and the development of the Seychelles' blue economy.

The creative sectors

Africa's creative sectors are gaining momentum thanks to the continent's young, creative talent: the film, television, radio, music, arts, design and fashion industries are thriving and attracting global interest like never before.

'Nollywood', the Nigerian film industry in Lagos, is the second-largest producer of films worldwide after India's Bollywood. More than 2,000 Nollywood films are made every year. It provides one million jobs, making it the largest employer in Nigeria after agriculture. Nollywood's annual turnover is approximately $800 million.[70]

Entertainment giants like Netflix and Warner Music Group are recognising the potential of the African music and film market as a source of talent and content and are actively seeking to capture a share of this market.[71]

African fashion is booming thanks to international buyers and increased demand from the continent's expanding urban middle class. Sub-Saharan Africa's $31 billion apparel sector is set to keep growing each year, and a fully developed industry would boost prosperity across the continent, potentially creating millions of jobs for women.[72]

African visual arts are flourishing like never before. The demand for contemporary African art, both from the affluent African middle class and from Europe and the United States, continues to increase. A BBC report showed that the value of African artefacts at art auctions is skyrocketing.[73] The work of contemporary African artists is gaining popularity in auction houses such as Sotheby's. This evolution offers more (especially young) African artists the opportunity to make a living from their work.

Creative industries currently contribute 3 per cent of the African GDP and have huge potential for growth and job creation. An additional layer in constructing more diverse and economically viable markets, they feed ecosystems involving artists, entrepreneurs, distributors and support services, and provide modern jobs. Access to technology and digital platforms is leveraging the sector's access to global markets across the continent and beyond.

The creative sectors are witnessing a cultural renaissance. African filmmakers, actors, writers, designers, musicians and other artists are not only an economic force but also contribute to preserving and promoting African cultural heritage and fostering social cohesion, both within the continent and globally.

African Entrepreneurship and Drive for Innovation

If Africa fails to create employment, it will certainly not be for a lack of work ethic or entrepreneurship. I am often impressed by the creativity, entrepreneurship and resilience of Africans.

African ingenuity

Clayton Christensen, a professor at Harvard Business School, believes that the key to economic development is the innovative capacity of African entrepreneurs creating their own market in an environment with low purchasing power. Traditional Western companies avoid this kind of environment because they believe that there is not enough purchasing power to be able to easily sell their products and services.[74] They do not invest in Africa because they see no buyers for their products. This is the opposite of entrepreneurs who 'develop market-creating innovations amid the nonconsumption that exists in many poor countries'.[75] They spot commercial opportunities that traditional Western companies do not see.

Africa has produced many of these innovative companies. Christensen shares the example of the Nigerian Tolaram, which sells small packages of instant noodles for $0.20. A traditional food company would never bring a product like this to market. Christensen believes the trick is to develop products that are cheap, simple and easily accessible. He sees a lot of potential for this in Africa. Tolaram now sells 4.5 billion bags of noodles a year, has invested more than $350 million in Nigeria and employs tens of thousands of people. But there are also examples of smaller companies that have been successful too. For Christensen, it is essential to allow that innovative capacity to flourish. This is more sustainable than enforcing development top-down.

It is fascinating that Ugandan refugee camps (where refugees are allowed to work, unlike in many other countries) have over time transformed into a kind of informal economic zone with huge markets made up of small businesses. Take, for example, the Nakivale camp in southwestern Uganda, where it is as if the informal economy appeared out of nowhere: a masterclass in creativity and inventiveness.

I had read about Nakivale in the book *Refuge* by Paul Collier and Alexander Betts.[76] Since I regularly travel to Uganda, as a director of the Finance Trust Bank, I decided to visit the Nakivale Refugee Settlement after a recent board meeting. The Ugandan government calls Nakivale a settlement and not a camp because the area is not fenced. Nakivale is situated in southwestern Uganda, a seven-hour drive from the capital Kampala, close to the borders with Congo and Rwanda. It is absolutely enormous, covering 185 km², and the oldest refugee settlement in the country. It was founded in 1958 to receive refugees from Rwanda. Paul Kagame, the current president of Rwanda, ended up in Nakivale when he was two years old. He later fought in the rebel army of Yoweri Museveni (now the president of Uganda) against the then dictator Milton Obote. Today, the settlement has 170,000 refugees, the vast majority of whom come from eastern Congo. The rest mainly come from Rwanda, Burundi, South Sudan, Ethiopia and Somalia. The settlement is jointly managed by the Ugandan government and the UN High Commissioner for Refugees (UNHCR). They outsource operational tasks, like education, health care, legal assistance and psychological support, to specialised NGOs. The refugees get a small amount of money each month (13,000 Ugandan shillings – about €3 – per person, including children). But they only receive it if they stay in the settlement. If they decide to move to the city, they lose their right to the allowance. Refugees in the settlement are also allocated a plot of land measuring 30 by 30 metres to build their own house (with building materials provided by the settlement) and to grow their own vegetables.

Innocent Asiimwe from the American NGO Alight[77] showed me around the settlement. The NGO encourages refugees to set up economic activities. For example, I met a savings and credit group with 20 members from Congo and Rwanda. Some of them reared goats, chickens or pigs. Others had opened a shop. They welcomed me into their modest homes, where I witnessed their suffering and sadness. Trying to find out if they still had family in their country of origin, I heard from one Congolese man that he had fled the violence in eastern Congo and that his family had been completely massacred. I will never forget the look of despair on his face. I then visited Nakivale's central market square, where the contrast could not have been greater.

This was what Paul Collier was no doubt referring to. The square was huge. It was teeming with market stalls selling all kinds of products: fruit and vegetables, meat, fish, clothing, pots and pans, drinks, oil and sauces, bread. Innocent took me to see a Congolese woman who had built a fully functional bakery and employed several young people. You could feel the positive energy here. They baked bread and biscuits to then sell all over the camp. Innocent explained to me that, for some, the post-traumatic stress is unbearable. Last year, Nakivale had 600 suicide attempts, a tenth of which were fatal. Others turn the page of the past and start a new life driven by creativity and entrepreneurship. The market sellers in Nakivale were a good illustration of this. One of the refugees had even started a taxi company providing regular rides to Kampala.

I also noticed that Ugandans talk about migrants and refugees in an empathetic way, even though Uganda has the largest number of refugees on the African continent. I asked Innocent whether that led to rivalry and tension with the local population. He replied that ordinary Ugandans do not think in terms of national borders, partly because in the past they too have fled. It doesn't matter where people come from. Innocent believes that community thinking (*ubuntu*) prevails. However, conflicts do arise around the settlement because the refugees are taking up more and more agricultural land.

At the end of my visit, I called into a library donated by an American philanthropist. It was a nice, neat room with well-stocked bookshelves and quiet areas to read in. On the shelves, I mainly saw textbooks: about the English language, about economics and management, geography, physics, mathematics and chemistry. A dozen young Africans were reading in complete silence. A young man came up to me and asked to speak to me, so we stepped outside. He was 20 years old and came from eastern Congo. He wanted to do everything he could to pursue a higher education. He asked me if I could help him. He didn't mind which subject he would study, but he wanted a dignified life and to leave the settlement. I wasn't able to give him an answer. The words and the desperation of this boy will stay with me forever.

What Is Needed to Create More Jobs?

Investment in education, training and development

Access to good-quality education, development and vocational training is essential for increasing the chances of young people in the labour market. Even though significant progress has been made in recent decades, African education lags behind the rest of the world. Only around 42 per cent of 15 to 24-year-olds in sub-Saharan Africa attended school until at least the end of lower secondary education (in principle until the age of 14–15 years). By comparison, in South Asia, school attendance is 82 per cent.[78] Sub-Saharan Africa has however managed to gradually improve the completion rate in primary education: from 54 per cent in 1990 to 70 per cent in 2023.[79]

Countless surveys show that increased education in Africa has come at the expense of quality. About 80 per cent of third-year primary school students in Mali and 70 per cent in Uganda are unable to read. Research into mathematical skills produced similar results.[80] Absenteeism among teachers is also very high, not least because they are poorly paid. Studies reveal teacher absenteeism rates of 16 to 20 per cent in Kenya, Senegal and Tanzania.[81]

The low level of education is also linked to the high cost of access to education. In many African countries, pupils have to pay school fees, even for primary education. While talking to microfinance bank customers, I discovered that families do everything they can to fund their children's education. For example, these families sometimes take out a loan to pay for it. The education and future of their children are the highest priority for the family budget.

Education is the key to a good job. There is a clear link between the level of education someone receives and the level of job they end up in. The majority of those who received only primary education eventually end up in small-scale family farming. Those who received a lower secondary education tend to end up in informal businesses. The vast majority of those who complete secondary education (or higher) become wage earners in the formal sector (companies and government).[82]

Education is not only essential for acquiring knowledge but also for developing socioemotional and behavioural skills, which are extremely important in our working lives. Furthermore, education also offers better insight into the way society works.

For each additional year of education received, subsequent income earned also increases more than proportionately. This is why it also makes sense for families to invest in their children's education: the economic return for the family is considerable.[83]

Professor Jeffrey Sachs emphasises that worldwide all young people up to the age of 18 should have the opportunity to attend school in line with Sustainable Development Goal #4. He believes that the budget expense for this must be covered by the international community. Achieving this worldwide would cost $39 billion per year.[84] Sachs compares that amount with the US defence budget (which amounted to around $840 billion in 2024).[85] He therefore calls for a reduction in the US defence budget in favour of access to education for all young people worldwide. This is an investment that would also support world peace, so the benefits for society are not to be underestimated. As a point of comparison, I believe that Europe should put a high priority on better African education. In the long term, financial support for education in Africa will probably contribute more to harmonious relationships between the two continents than investments in Frontex, the European Border and Coast Guard Agency.

Education up to the age of 18 also influences the position of women and demography. Sachs points to the importance of compulsory schooling for girls up to the age of 18. Research has shown that in the short term this reduces the birth rate by 10 per cent[86] because it leads to young women delaying having their first child.

Given the low level of education, specialists see a key role for second-chance education and vocational training. In Africa, it is often private companies that offer this training. In several African countries (including Kenya), the government provides vouchers to young people that they can then use to follow training courses in the private sector. These voucher programmes have proven to be successful and can also offer a way to give women better access to training.[87]

An evidence-based report from UNICEF and the African Union on the situation of education in Africa[88] acknowledges that Africa has made substantial progress in getting children to school. But despite the progress, the report also highlights major challenges. (1) There are still too many children on the margins of education (41 per cent of primary- and secondary-age children are out of school). (2) Poor learning outcomes remain a challenge. Nearly 87 per cent of children are unable to read and understand a simple text by the age of 10. (3) Africa is facing a serious deficit in qualified teachers. The continent will need 17 million additional teachers in order to achieve universal primary and secondary education by 2030. Therefore, the report urges governments to transform education in Africa.

Fewer trade barriers

Countless intra-African trade barriers are severely hampering potential economic growth, especially in the agricultural sector. Until recently, Africa had the highest import duties in the world, including between African countries.[89]

There are also a lot of non-tariff trade barriers within Africa, such as customs formalities. For example, completing the customs formalities to import a container into Congo takes an average of fifty days.[90]

Trade between African countries amounts to only 15 per cent of all African foreign trade (some say 40 per cent if you also count smuggling and informal trade flows[91]). Either way, that is a low percentage compared to intracontinental trade in Asia (61 per cent) or Europe (67 per cent).[92] African trade mainly consists of exports of primary commodities to the rest of the world.[93]

African governments are aware of the problem. In 2018, the members of the African Union concluded the treaty establishing the African Continental Free Trade Area (AfCFTA), which aims to promote intra-regional trade in Africa. The treaty provides for a range of measures aimed at not only reducing or eliminating import tariffs and other trade barriers between African states but also improving infrastructure and aligning national legislation (for example, on competition policy or intellectual property). Under the new agreement, free trade was introduced in 2021.[94] But it will still be years before the entire agreement is implemented. Despite this, it is a very important and optimistic agreement that provides Africa with the tools to create more intracontinental trade.

Sub-regional economic partnerships that pursue these objectives on a smaller scale have actually already existed for some time. The most important of these are the Southern African Development Community (SADC), founded in 1980, which brings together 16 countries from southern Africa, and the Economic Community of West African States (ECOWAS), founded in 1975, which includes 15 countries from West Africa. However, in 2024, Niger, Burkina Faso and Mali withdrew from ECOWAS after military coups in these countries. It is the AfCFTA's responsibility to coordinate and accelerate the work of these sub-regional partnerships.

Research shows that the range of exportable African products, excluding raw materials, is rather limited. This is a fundamental problem that will not be solved by removing trade barriers.[95] Trade flows between African countries can grow fastest through increased trade in agricultural products. One of the goals of the previously mentioned Malabo Declaration of 2014 was to triple intra-African trade in these agricultural products.

Any discussion on African trade policy needs to include an analysis of the infamous Economic Partnership Agreements (EPAs), something that has caused a lot of commotion in the past. The EPAs replaced the Lomé (1975) and Cotonou (2020) agreements, which from 1975 ensured that the African, Caribbean and Pacific (ACP) countries had preferential access to European markets. However, the agreements did not comply with the non-discrimination principle of the World Trade Organization (WTO), established in 1995. From 2002 onwards, the EU started negotiating with the various sub-regional trading blocs in Africa.[96] Although the original intention was to mutually reduce tariffs, the EU – under pressure from the ACP countries – gradually agreed to conclude so-called asymmetric agreements: African products get free access to European markets, but the tariff barriers to the import of European products into Africa will only be gradually reduced over a period of fifteen to twenty years. There are some exceptions, for example, imports of European agricultural products that will remain subject to import duties.[97] There are now seven different sub-regional EPAs, some of which are still in the process of being ratified by individual states.[98]

The EPAs have received a lot of criticism, primarily from Africa. Nigeria's manufacturing industry put up a fierce resistance, fearing that European imports would destroy their emerging local industry. The young Nigerian pharmaceutical industry, among others, shared their concern.[99] In Senegal, the dairy industry feared that cheap French milk powder would cripple the fragile local dairy industry. Earlier, I described the impact of increased imports of European dairy products on local milk production in West Africa. But this was due to the scrapping of European milk quotas and not the result of the EPAs.

Studies have attempted to highlight the impact of the EPAs on the African economy. In some countries, this has been both negative and positive.[100] The so-called 'least developed countries'[101] can export to the EU without tariff barriers.[102] The EPAs have not changed this. The EPAs have also included other states on the list of countries with preferential access to EU markets. Before the EPAs, they already enjoyed preferential access to the EU markets under the Lomé and Cotonou agreements but saw their privileges challenged by the WTO. The EPAs provide for the fact that these countries will also be guaranteed free access in the future, and that is positive. Since the obligation to reduce African import tariffs for products from Europe is only being rolled out gradually and excludes agricultural products in the broader sense, the possible negative impact on local African companies due to the increase of imports from Europe appears to be limited.

EPAs do, however, have a negative impact on the budgets of African states, as they mean that over time these countries can collect fewer import duties.[103]

According to the EU, one of the key objectives of the EPAs was to better integrate the African economy into the global economy. Researchers have also observed little to no effect here.[104] The reason again is that a lot of African companies do not have the required capacity to participate competitively in the global economy. That objective seems not to have taken into account the reality on the ground and was more of a way of making the EPAs politically palatable.

Ultimately, the impact of the EPAs for Africa – both the feared disadvantages and the sought-after benefits – is limited. The good news is that the African Union is tackling the trade issue itself and is working on a large internal African market.

Investment in infrastructure and energy supplies

When it comes to roads, railways, ports, airports, electricity grids, water distribution networks, sewerage systems and the internet, Africa's infrastructure is lagging behind. This not only compromises the quality of life for Africans but also slows down economic activity.

Due to a supply failure, 300 million Africans do not have access to drinking water. And some 700 million Africans do not have access to sanitation,[105] which leads to serious health problems.

Furthermore, 600 million Africans do not have access to electricity, a major inconvenience for countless families. Companies often – for lack of any alternative – resort to polluting diesel-powered generators, the electricity for which costs three to six times more than regular mains electricity.[106] Furthermore, the power supply often cuts out due to poor maintenance of the power plants. By the side of the road in Guinea, I saw countless small metal companies producing iron gates and fences. Grid overloads causing daytime power outages meant that they had to do all their welding at night.

Nevertheless, Africa has enormous potential for renewable energy from hydropower and solar energy. In Kenya, renewables already account for 90 per cent of energy produced and consumed.[107] Only 11 per cent of the hydropower potential of the continent is currently being used. Meanwhile, solar energy is on the rise. No other continent has more potential for solar energy. The number of small-scale off-grid solar panels, which even serve families in rural areas, is steadily increasing. Large-scale solar parks are also being built.[108]

Some people believe that sub-Saharan Africa offers the ideal environment for the (energy-intensive) production of 'green' hydrogen, because the continent can rely on cheap photovoltaic energy production. Green hydrogen, a 'clean' energy carrier, has a role to play in our planet's much-needed energy transition.[109] Others are sceptical because the transport costs of hydrogen are very high and because the production and conversion of hydrogen incur significant efficiency losses.

The road network is also lacking. Only a quarter of Africa's roads are paved.[110] In some countries, rural roads are inaccessible to vehicles, especially freight traffic. This means that small farmers in rural areas often have difficulty transporting their fresh produce to the markets in the cities. The existing road network is saturated and no longer fit for purpose. Our traffic jams are nothing compared to those in African cities like Lagos, Kampala, Kinshasa and Nairobi. In addition, heavy soot emissions from third-hand cars and lorries often rejected by Europe make the air highly polluted and unbearable.

Investment in drinking water

In 2023, Incofin established the Water Access Acceleration Fund (W2AF), an investment fund for small companies that produce drinking water. Since public infrastructure in the Global South is often inadequate (for example, because public water pipes are only available in certain parts of big cities), the last decade has seen numerous initiatives by entrepreneurs to produce and distribute drinking water via so-called water kiosks: a network of distribution points that sell drinking water at a publicly accessible tap or in reusable bottles. The water kiosks produce their own water by pumping it up and then purifying it. These companies distribute the water at an affordable price and a fraction of what you would pay for bottled water in shops.

W2AF primarily invests in Africa and Asia, in regions where no coverage is provided by public drinking water companies. A €70 million fund, W2AF aims to make a modest financial return. The fund's main goal is to provide water to as many people as possible. Once all investments have been made, W2AF will be providing approximately 30 million people with access to drinking water.

Mobile phones

One area where African infrastructure is efficient is mobile phone networks: 63 in 100 Africans have a mobile phone.[111] Mobile networks have revolutionised payment systems and app development has become a booming new, innovative industry. Apps are being developed in various sectors. In Kenya, I saw how milk collection from small farmers was controlled entirely by apps, leading to faster and more accurate payment.

Investments in infrastructure

Serious efforts are being made to improve the quality of Africa's infrastructure. In 2018, infrastructure investments exceeded $100 billion for the first time in African history. That is a third more than in the period 2015–2017[112] and three times as much as in the early twenty-first century.[113] The investment amount fell in 2019 and 2020 to $85 and $81 billion respectively, partly due to the Covid pandemic.

In 2010, the African Union developed a long-term programme for the development of African infrastructure.[114] The programme runs until 2040 and includes $360 billion in investments, mainly in energy and transport. The African Development Bank is responsible for coordinating the programme.

Where does the money for infrastructure investments come from? The financing mainly comes in the form of loans, not donations. An international consortium has mapped out the financing flows for the whole of Africa (both North Africa and sub-Saharan Africa).[115] In 2020, African governments funded 41 per cent of projects. Having provided 26 per cent of the financing in 2018, Chinese investments fell to 7.4 per cent in 2020. This is because China is treading more carefully as a result of defaults it has experienced in African countries. Europe accounts for just 4.5 per cent of the funding. Over the years, the private sector has become an important player, contributing 23.4 per cent of all financing.

In addition to large-scale infrastructure, small, targeted investments are also very important. A very simple measure, for example, is to improve marketplaces used by small market sellers. I have often walked around African markets and sometimes they are so badly maintained that you can barely make your way through them. Or they are very unsanitary and dirty. In some cities, the government has put a lot of effort into modernising the markets to attract more buyers and generate a higher turnover for the market sellers. This is what happened in, for example, Dar es Salaam, the capital of Tanzania, where the government, together with the NGO GAIN, completely modernised the Buguruni market. This made the market a more hygienic, efficient and attractive place for small traders and their customers.[116]

Revenues from mining

Mining could certainly contribute to Africa's prosperity if mining companies behaved responsibly and governments used the profits from mining concessions in the public's interest. In Norway, petroleum and gas revenues are saved in a sovereign fund. Botswana set up something similar in 1993 for the proceeds of diamond production. However, too many African rulers still use the income from mining for their own benefit. Or they sell mining concessions at bargain-basement prices to shady parties, who then share part of the profit with those in power.

Erik Bruyland has provided a detailed account of how this works in the copper and cobalt mining industry in Congo.[117] For example, cobalt concessions in Congo were dubiously acquired by Switzerland-based Glencore.[118] The company used all kinds of constructions to share its profits – especially during the Kabila period – with the highest authorities in the country, who in turn facilitated the acquisition of the concessions by Glencore. On top of that, cobalt is mined not only through established mining companies but also in an uncontrolled manner by artisanal *creuseurs* in inhumane conditions and sold at bargain-basement prices to unscrupulous intermediaries.

The responsibility of successive Congolese rulers, Joseph Kabila in particular, is astounding. But the behaviour of some of the foreign companies involved (Swiss, Canadian, American, Chinese) is also downright immoral. Not to mention their lack of respect for decent working conditions and environmental standards. Europe has taken a positive step by introducing legislation that requires European companies to map out the supply chains of conflict minerals and monitor their risks from 2021 onwards.

The sector is in urgent need of transformation to make a positive contribution to African society. And African leaders are the only ones who can enforce such change.

An excellent example of positive change is a recent venture between the Belgian company Umicore and STL, a subsidiary of Gécamines, the Congolese state-owned mining company. In 2024, they agreed on a long-term partnership whereby Umicore will support STL to valorise germanium from its site in Lubumbashi. Umicore will optimise STL's new processing facility at the site, using its refining and recycling expertise in return for exclusive access to the processed germanium in order to produce material solutions for high-tech applications.[119]

Conclusion: Where will jobs come from?

Based on the above, I will now provide a summary of the eight sectors where I see ample potential for job growth in Africa. It would be reckless, however, to venture into quantitative estimates.

1. Agri-food is perhaps the most powerful catalyst for job creation. The growing demand for food, both from Africa itself and from the rest of the world, can make this sector an even greater source of employment. The Nigerian company Flour Mills of Nigeria has until now produced flour from wheat imported from the United States. Currently, the company is supporting a programme to source wheat from Nigerian smallholder farmers. Imagine what would happen if Africa replaced its imports of agricultural products ($43 billion per year) with locally produced commodities. The same applies, as mentioned earlier, to the export of raw cocoa beans from Ivory Coast and Ghana. These beans can easily be processed locally rather than being shipped in raw form to the rest of the world. Furthermore, the agri-food sector can enhance its appeal by investing in technology, which will draw a greater number of young people to the field. This is happening in India, for example. Private and public investment funds can accelerate the growth of the sector by financing innovative investments.

2. Africa's critical raw materials are essential for our planet's energy transition and for all kinds of high-tech applications. Today, raw materials are mined in African mines and then transported to the nearest port to be shipped from there to Europe, the United States, China and other areas. There is not a lot of benefit from this mine-to-port approach for the African economy. That is why it is important that critical and other raw materials are also processed locally. The Congolese government hopes to one day produce batteries locally using Congolese cobalt. Morocco, although not in sub-Saharan Africa, will produce one million EVs (electric vehicles) in 2025, an inspiring example for the rest of the continent. Or perhaps African governments can take inspiration from the Indonesian government, which grants Chinese, Korean and Japanese companies access to Indonesian nickel and cobalt on the condition that they invest in local processing plants in Indonesia. The job potential of the African raw materials sector is enormous. Only a proactive approach by African governments will lead to more jobs.

3. The African economy has been undergoing a shift to services over the past 20 years, as people have taken more jobs in finance, trade and other

services in cities. Employment in the service sector increased from 30 per cent to 39 per cent over that period.[120] In addition to the growth of the financial sector, the expansion of IT companies stands out. We mentioned earlier that IT companies from Africa provide services to the rest of the world. The potential lies in the fact that Africa's well-trained middle class could meet the growing global talent shortage via services outsourcing.

4. Africa has over 40 per cent of the world's renewable energy resources. In the last decade, only $60 billion or 2 per cent of all $3 trillion renewable energy investments worldwide were channelled to Africa. During the African Union's first Africa Climate Summit of September 2023, African leaders called on the global community to boost climate-positive investments in Africa.[121] Kenya is leading the way. As mentioned, the country relies on renewables for roughly 90 per cent of its power supply.[122] Kenya's electricity generation grew by 4.9 per cent a year on average during the last decade, driven by major investment from both the public and the foreign private sectors in geothermal and wind power, and more recently in solar power. Off-grid solar is also booming in Kenya. Grid-generation capacity doubled in 2013–2022, from 1,800 MW to 3,600 MW, while electricity production, in GWh, climbed by 51 per cent. A switch in the main source of baseload power from hydroelectricity to geothermal – tapping steam resources in the Rift Valley – means the system is now more stable and drought resistant. The Kenyan example can be an inspiration for many other African countries. Kenya's decentralised renewable energy sector on its own accounts for 50,000 jobs.[123]

5. A lot of infrastructure works are under construction or being planned in the coming years and decades. We have already seen the ambitious plans of the African Union to invest billions in infrastructure: the so-called Programme for Infrastructure Development in Africa (PIDA), a programme monitored by the African Union for enhancing continental connectivity in transport, energy, ICT and transboundary water resources. In recent years, between $80 billion and $100 billion worth of infrastructure works have been approved annually. These infrastructure works provide a lot of jobs. Since foreign powers see a role for themselves in the financing and delivery of large infrastructure works in Africa (see also Chapter 5) and these are of strategic importance to them, African governments can leverage this foreign interest to realise a maximum number of works at a minimum price with a maximum employment impact.

6. Earlier we explored the job potential of the blue economy, in particular tourism. It is certainly crucial to prioritise the promotion of ecotourism.

7. Even though the creative industries we described are still relatively small today, this sector has a bright future with many jobs ahead of it.
8. Africa boasts some great assets as guardian of the biodiversity of our planet. The tropical rainforest is home to a wealth of biodiversity. The Parties to the Convention on Biological Diversity (a collection of 196 countries) have set ambitious biodiversity targets. Until now, loss of habitats or ecosystems has been frequently addressed through biodiversity offsetting. Experts are increasingly in favour of a new framework for compensating for biodiversity losses in a way that is aligned with biodiversity targets. They propose a financial ecological compensation that is appropriate for contributing to the achievement of biodiversity targets. Smallholder farmers maintaining the tropical rainforest could be financially recognised for their efforts and for refraining from expanding fields and cutting down woodland. Experiments are underway and, although it is still early days, the system of ecological compensations seems very promising for anyone who actively contributes to biodiversity and whose efforts currently go unrecognised. There is potential for a new economic sector to emerge here.

The African economy has opportunities to offer meaningful and dignified jobs to more and more people. But the influx into the labour market over the coming decades will be so big that new jobs in the sectors described above will not, even in the most optimistic scenario, be able to absorb the surplus in labour. With its millions of household enterprises and small farmers, the informal economy will therefore act as a safety net for the labour market for a long time to come. It is important to realise that the informal economy will remain a cornerstone of the African economy. This sector therefore deserves continued support. This is what I will explore in the next chapter.

Notes

1 Aidar Abdychev, Cristian Alonso, Emre Alper et al., 'The Future of Work in Sub-Saharan Africa'. IMF, African Department No. 18/18 (2018), 5–7.
2 World Bank Group, Data. Accessed 8 January 2025. https://data.worldbank.org/indicator/SL.EMP.TOTL.SP.ZS?locations=ZG. Employment rate defined as the share of working population in relation to the total population over the age of 15 years old.
3 World Bank Group, Data. Accessed 8 January 2025. https://data.worldbank.org/indicator/SL.UEM.TOTL.ZS?locations=ZG. Unemployment as a percentage of the labour force. Figure for 2023.

4 World Bank Group, Data. Accessed 8 January 2025. https://data.worldbank
.org/indicator/SL.EMP.SELF.ZS?locations=ZG&view=chart. Figure for
2022.

5 W. Arthur Lewis, 'Economic Development with Unlimited Supplies of Labor'.
The Manchester School, May 1954. 'Productivity' is measured here in economic
terms as 'added value per person'.

6 Mayowa Kuyoro, Acha Leke, Olivia White, et al., *Reimagining Economic Growth
in Africa – Turning Diversity into Opportunity* (McKinsey Global Institute, June
2023), 17. The figures are for the whole of Africa, including the Maghreb
countries. Admittedly, it is not clear whether the service sector in the report
includes both formal and informal businesses.

7 Jacques Bughin, Mutsa Chironga, Georges Desvaux, et al., *Lions on the Move
II: Realizing the Potential of Africa's Economies* (McKinsey Global Institute,
September 2016).

8 Carlos Lopes and George Kararach, *Structural Change in Africa: Misperceptions,
New Narratives and Development in the 21st Century* (Routledge, 2020), 89.

9 Nicole Kearse, Bogolo Kenewendo, Jakaya Mrisho Kikwete, et al., *Top
Priorities for the Continent in 2023: Foresight Africa* (Africa Growth Initiative at
Brookings, 2023), 42.

10 Louise Fox and Thomas S. Jayne, 'Unpacking the Misconceptions About
Africa's Food Imports'. *Brookings Commentary,* 14 December 2020. Accessed 8
January 2025. https://www.brookings.edu/articles/unpacking-the-miscon-
ceptions-about-africas-food-imports/.

11 Lopes and Kararach, *Structural Change in Africa: Misperceptions, New Narratives
and Development in the 21st Century,* 26.

12 There are also batteries without cobalt: LFP batteries.

13 Fairtrade Risk Map. Accessed 8 January 2025. https://riskmap.fairtrade.net/
commodities/cocoa. .

14 Reuters, 'Ivory Coast to Boost Cocoa Processing with 2 New Factories'. 22
September 2020. Accessed 8 January 2025. https://www.reuters.com/article
/idUSL5N2GJ4DY/.

15 Jan Grumiller and Werner Raza, *The Ethiopian Leather and Leather Products Sector:
An Assessment of Export Potentials to Europe and Austria,* Austrian Foundation for
Development Research, Research Report 11/2019.

16 World Bank Group, Data. Accessed 8 January 2025. https://data.worldbank
.org/indicator/SL.AGR.EMPL.ZS?locations=ZG. Numbers for 2022.

17 World Bank Group, Data. Accessed 8 January 2025. https://data.worldbank
.org/indicator/NV.AGR.TOTL.ZS?locations=ZG. Number for 2023.

18 Lopes and Kararach, *Structural Change in Africa: Misperceptions, New Narratives
and Development in the 21st Century,* 33.

19 Ibid., 20.

20 Ibid., 7.

21 Kristina Sokourenko, Lawrence Haddad, Ty Beal, Vine Mutyasira, and
Boaz Keizire, 'African Food Systems a Regional, Data-based Snapshot'.
Gain Briefing Paper N°9, December 2022. https://www.gainhealth.org/sites
/default/files/publications/documents/GAIN-Briefing-Paper-series-9-africa
-food-systems.pdf.

22 Conference of Ministers of Agriculture of the African Union, 'Report of the Ministers of Agriculture'. Maputo, 1–2 July 2003. https://openknowledge.fao .org/server/api/core/bitstreams/22f80d3a-40e0-491a-bdf7-6f76b1b4f937/ content/ad121e.htm.

23 Heads of State and Government of the African Union, 'Malabo Declaration on Accelerated Agricultural Growth and Transformation for Shared Prosperity and Improved Livelihoods'. *Malabo, Equatorial Guinea*, 26–27 June 2014.

24 Suwadu Sakho-Jimbira and Ibrahima Hathie, 'The Future of Agriculture in Sub-Saharan Africa'. *Southern Voice*, Policy Brief No. 2, April 2020, 2. Accessed 8 January 2025. https://southernvoice.org/the-future-of-agriculture-in-sub -saharan-africa/.

25 Philippe Lebailly, Michel Baudouin, and Roger Ntoto, 'Quel développement agricole pour la RDC?' In *Conjonctures Congolaises 2014: politiques, territoires et ressources naturelles: changements et continuités*, edited by Stefaan Marysse and Jean Omasombo Tshonda (Éditions L'Harmattan, 2015), 51.

26 Ibid., 57. Translated from the French.

27 Lewis, 'Economic Development with Unlimited Supplies of Labor'.

28 'Ankole Coffee Producers' Cooperative Union Limited'. Accessed 8 January 2025. https://www.acpcultd.com/.

29 Deon Filmer and Louise Fox, 'Youth Employment in Sub-Saharan Africa'. Africa Development Series (World Bank. 2014), 11–13. doi:10.1596/978-1-4648-0107-5.

30 Sarah K. Lowder, Jakob Skoet, and Terri Raney, 'The Number, Size and Distribution of Farms, Smallholder Farms and Family Farms Worldwide'. *World Development*, Vol. 87, 2016, 16–29. http://dx.doi.org/10.1016/j.worlddev .2015.10.041.

31 AUC/OECD, *Africa's Development Dynamics 2023: Investing in Sustainable Development* (AUC- OECD Publishing, 2023), 64. https://doi.org/10.1787 /3269532b-en.

32 The Economist, 'African Pension Funds Have Grown Impressively'. 2 October 2021. https://www.economist.com/middle-east-and-africa/2021/10 /02/african-pension-funds-have-grown-impressively.

33 Paul Vossen, *Jullie rijkdom en onze beschaving: de onzin van de koloniale ruil* (Skribis, 2021), 149. Sub-Saharan Africa has the most oxisol and ultisol soils in the world.

34 Vossen, *Jullie rijkdom en onze beschaving: de onzin van de koloniale ruil*, 167. Namely, 5,995 kg/ha in Western Europe compared to 2,889 kg/ha in sub-Saharan Africa.

35 G. Duteurtre, C. Corniaux, and A. De Palmas, 'Milk, Trade and Development in the Sahel: Socioeconomic and Environmental Impacts of European Vegetable Fat Dairy Blend Imports in West Africa'. Report for the "Greens" and "S&D" Groups of the European Parliament (CIRAD, 2021). https://agri-trop.cirad.fr/597139CIRAD.

36 Filmer and Fox, 'Youth Employment in Sub-Saharan Africa'.

37 Agnes Andersson Djurfeldt, Fred Mawunyo Dzanku, and Aida Cuthbert Isinika, *Agriculture, Diversification and Gender in Rural Africa: Longitudinal Perspectives from Six Countries* (Oxford University Press, 2018), 19.

38 African Union, 'Declaration on Land Issues and Challenges in Africa'. Assembly/AU/Decl.1(XIII) Rev.1, 2009.

39 African Development Bank Group, African Natural Resource Centre, *Rethinking Land Reform in Africa New Ideas, Opportunities, and Challenges* (ANRC-AfDB, 2020), 17.

40 Sophie Edwards and Madalitso Wills Kateta, 'Malawi Land Reforms Spark Controversy, Fear of Lost Investment'. *Devex*, 2 May 2023. Accessed 8 January 2025. https://www.devex.com/news/malawi-land-reforms-spark-controversy -fear-of-lost-investment-105423.

41 Ann Wavinya, 'Transforming Smallholder Farms Through Soil Health Data'. *World Agroforestry*, 30 March 2023. Accessed 8 January 2025. https://world-agroforestry.org/blog/2023/03/30/transforming-smallholder-farms-through -soil-health-data?kid=2542.

42 Ronny Swennen, 'Our Goal Is to Find a Whole Range of Climate-smart Bananas'. KU Leuven, Department of Biosystems, 29 January 2020. Accessed 8 January 2025. https://www.biw.kuleuven.be/biosyst/english/archives/our -goal-is-to-find-a-whole-range-of-climate-smart-bananas.

43 Vossen, *Jullie rijkdom en onze beschaving: de onzin van de koloniale ruil*, 190. Translated from the Dutch.

44 Filmer and Fox, 'Youth Employment in Sub-Saharan Africa', 130.

45 Djurfeldt, Dzanku, and Isinika, *Agriculture, Diversification and Gender in Rural Africa: Longitudinal Perspectives from Six Countries*, 19.

46 Ibid., 120.

47 Filmer and Fox, 'Youth Employment in Sub-Saharan Africa', 133.

48 Djurfeldt, Dzanku, and Isinika, *Agriculture, Diversification and Gender in Rural Africa: Longitudinal Perspectives from Six Countries*, 83.

49 Geetha Nagarajan and Richard L. Meyer, 'Rural Finance: Recent Advances and Emerging Lessons, Debates, and Opportunities'. Reformatted version of Working Paper AEDE-WP-0041-05, Department of Agricultural, Environmental, and Development Economics (The Ohio State University, 2005).

50 Incofin IM, 'RIF II Environmental & Social Closing Report: Moving the Frontier of Microfinance to Rural Areas: Ten Years Later'. Internal Incofin IM Paper (2021), 7.

51 African Union, African Development Bank, United Nations Economic Commission for Africa, 'Guiding Principles on Large Scale Land Based Investments in Africa' (2014).

52 Marie-France Cros, 'RD Congo: l'inspection des impôts dénonce la disparition de 205 millions de dollars à Bukanga Lonzo'. *La Libre Afrique*, 19 November 2020. Accessed 9 January 2025. https://afrique.lalibre.be/55868 /rdcongo-linspection-des-impots-denonce-la-disparition-de-205-millions-de -dollars-a-bukanga-lonzo/.

53 Food and Agriculture Organization of the United Nations, *The State of Food and Agriculture: Innovation in Family Farming* (FAO, 2014), 3.

54 Ibid., 29.

55 Ibid., 3.

56 'Great Green Wall'. Accessed 9 January 2025. https://thegreatgreenwall.org/ about-great-green-wall.

57 Filmer and Fox, 'Youth Employment in Sub-Saharan Africa', 153 (figures from 2014).
58 Ibid., 153.
59 Ibid., 160.
60 Pesa is Swahili for 'money'. The name 'M-Pesa' refers to mobile money.
61 William Cook and Claudia McKay, 'Banking in the M-Pesa Age: Lessons from Kenya'. Consultative Group to Assist the Poor Working Paper September 2017, 1.
62 'M-Pesa'. Accessed 9 January 2025. www.vodafone.com/what-we-do/services/m-pesa.
63 'Next Einstein Forum'. Accessed 9 January 2025. https://nef.org/about/.
64 'Amalitech'. Accessed 9 January 2025. https://amalitech.com/.
65 United Nations Commission for Africa, *Africa's Blue Economy: A Policy Handbook* (Economic Commission for Africa, 2016), Foreword.
66 Lopes and Kararach, *Structural Change in Africa: Misperceptions, New Narratives and Development in the 21st Century*, 113.
67 African Union – Inter-African Bureau for Animal Resources, *Africa Blue Economy Strategy* (AU-IBAR, 2019).
68 World Bank Group, 'Blue Economy in Africa: A Synthesis – Blue Economy for Resilient Africa Program'. Operational Brief (2022).
69 World Bank Group, 'Seychelles Launches World's First Sovereign Blue Bond'. Press Release, 20 October 2018. Accessed 9 January 2025. https://www.worldbank.org/en/news/press-release/2018/10/29/seychelles-launches-worlds-first-sovereign-blue-bond.
70 Lopes and Kararach, *Structural Change in Africa: Misperceptions, New Narratives and Development in the 21st Century*, 118.
71 Angela Lusigi, 'Accelerating Creativity and Innovation in Africa'. *UNDP Ghana Blog,* 21 April 2023. Accessed 9 January 2025. https://www.undp.org/ghana/blog/accelerating-creativity-and-innovation-africa.
72 Louise Donovan, 'African Fashion Is Booming. It Could Create Millions of Jobs for Women'. The Fuller Project – Groundbreaking Reporting on Women, 6 November 2023. Accessed 9 January 2025. https://fullerproject.org/story/african-fashion-is-booming-it-could-create-millions-of-jobs-for-women/.
73 Egon Cossou, 'African Contemporary Art Enjoying a Surge in interest'. *BBC,* 13 October 2022. Accessed 9 January 2025. https://www.bbc.com/news/business-63200559.
74 Clayton M. Christensen, Efosa Ojomoa, and Karen Dillon, *The Prosperity Paradox: How Innovation Can Lift Nations Out of Poverty* (HarperCollins, 2019).
75 Ibid., 67.
76 Alexander Betts and Paul Collier, *Refuge: Rethinking Refugee Policy in a Changing World* (Oxford University Press, 2017), 162.
77 'Alight'. Accessed 9 January 2025. https://www.wearealight.org/who-we-are.
78 UNESCO, 'World Inequality Database on Education'. Accessed 9 January 2025. https://www.education-inequalities.org/indicators/comp_lowsec_v2#ageGroup=%22comp_lowsec_v2%22&sortMode=%22mean%22&dimension=%7B%22id%22%3A%22sex%222C%22filters%223A%5B%5D%7D&countries=%5B%5D&minYear=2020&maxYear=2023.

79 World Bank Group Data. Accessed 9 January 2025. https://data.worldbank
.org/indicator/SE.PRM.CMPT.ZS?locations=ZG&view=chart.
80 Filmer and Fox, 'Youth Employment in Sub-Saharan Africa', 76.
81 Ibid., 80.
82 Ibid., 69.
83 Ibid., 72.
84 Education for All Global Monitoring Report, 'Pricing the Right to Education
– the Cost of Reaching New Targets by 2030'. Policy Paper 18, July 2015
(Unesco, 2015).
85 Jeffrey Sachs, 'Financing Health and Education for All'. United Nations
Sustainable Development Goals, Sachs Op-ed, 31 May 2016. Accessed 9
January 2025. https://www.un.org/sustainabledevelopment/blog/2016/05/
sachs-op-ed-financing-health-and-education-for-all/.
86 Quentin Wodon, Chata Male, Adenike Onagoruwa, and Ali Yedan, 'Girls'
Education and Child Marriage in West and Central Africa: Key Findings
ahead of the October 2017 High-Level Meeting on Ending Child Marriage
in West and Central Africa'. In *Girls' Education and Child Marriage in West and
Central Africa Notes Series*. Education Global Practice (The World Bank, 2017).
87 Filmer and Fox, 'Youth Employment in Sub-Saharan Africa', 94–102.
88 UNICEF and African Union, 'Transforming Education in Africa:
An Evidence-based Overview and Recommendations for Long-term
Improvements – A Report by UNICEF and the African Union Commission'
(2021).
89 The average import tax between African countries in 2010 was 8.6 per cent
of the value of the imported goods (Europe: 0 per cent). For agricultural products, the average tax was as high as 15.2 per cent (Europe: 0 per cent). Source:
Antoine Boüet, Lionel Cosnard and David Laborde, 'Measuring Trade
Integration in Africa'. International Food Research Policy Institute, *IFPRI
Discussion Paper 01667* (2017), 11.
90 Boüet, Cosnard, and Laborde, 'Measuring Trade Integration in Africa', 25.
91 This percentage is quoted in an article in *The Economist* ('African Trade: Deals
on Wheels', 28 January 2023).
92 United Nations Conference on Trade and Development, *Economic Development
in Africa – Report 2019* (UNCTAD, 2019), 20. Figures refer to the period
2015–2017.
93 Ibid., 24.
94 African Union, 'Agreement Establishing the African Continental Free Trade
Area', 29–30 January 2012. https://au.int/en/treaties/agreement-establish-
ing-african-continental-free-trade-area.
95 Boüet, Cosnard, and Laborde, 'Measuring Trade Integration in Africa', 5.
96 European Parliament, 'An Overview of the EU-ACP's Economic Partnership
Agreements – Building a New Trade Relationship'. European Parliament
Briefing (2018). Accessed 9 January 2025. https://www.europarl.europa.eu/
thinktank/en/document/EPRS_BRI(2018)625102.
97 Ibid., 6.
98 European Commission, *Overview of Economic Partnership Agreements – Update
March 2021* (Brussels, 2021).

99   'EPA: Enslavement Partnership Agreement?'. *Vanguard*, September 2017. https://www.vanguardngr.com/2017/09/epa-enslavement-partnership-agreement-2/.

100 Antoine Boüet, David Laborde, and Fousseini Traoré, 'The European Union–West Africa Economic Partnership Agreement: Small Impact and New Questions'. IFPRI Discussion Paper 01612 (Washington, DC: International Food Policy Research Institute, February 2017).

101 The OECD ranks all countries in the world according to their income levels. The list of the poorest countries on the planet (the least developed countries or LDCs) includes 45 countries, of which 32 are African countries (see Accessed 9 January 2025. https://www.oecd.org/en/topics/oda-eligibility-and-conditions/dac-list-of-oda-recipients.html#oda-recipients-list).

102 European Commission, 'Everything but Arms (EBA)'. *Access2Markets*. Accessed 9 January 2025. https://trade.ec.europa.eu/access-to-markets/en/content/everything-arms-eba.

103 European Parliament, 'An Overview of the EU-ACP's Economic Partnership Agreements – Building a New Trade Relationship', 102.

104 Sean Woolfrey and San Bilal, 'The Impact of Economic Partnership Agreements on the Development of African Value Chains'. *ECDPM Discussion Paper,* no 213 (2017), 26–28.

105 The Infrastructure Consortium for Africa, 'Water'. Accessed 10 January 2025. https://www.icafrica.org/en/topics-programmes/water/.

106 McKinsey & Company, *Solving Africa's Infrastructure Paradox*, 6 March 2020.

107 International Energy Agency, 'Energy Efficiency for Affordability: Executive Summary'. Accessed 10 January 2025. https://www.iea.org/reports/energy-efficiency-for-affordability/executive-summary.

108 International Energy Agency, *Africa Energy Outlook 2019* (Paris, 2020), 72–73.

109 Francesco La Camera, *The Geopolitics of the Energy Transformation: The Hydrogen Factor* (International Renewable Energy Agency, 2022).

110 African Development Bank Group, *African Economic Outlook 2019* (Abidjan, 2019), 101.

111 The Infrastructure Consortium for Africa, 'ICT'. Accessed 10 January 2025. https://www.icafrica.org/en/topics-programmes/ict/.

112 The Infrastructure Consortium for Africa, 'Key Achievements in the Financing of African Infrastructure in 2019–2020'. Accessed 10 January 2025. https://www.icafrica.org/en/topics-programmes/key-achievements-in-the-financing-of-african-infrastructure-in-2019-2020/.

113 McKinsey & Company, *Solving Africa's Infrastructure Paradox*, 6 March 2020.

114 The investment programme's name is PIDA (The Programme for Infrastructure Development in Africa).

115 The Infrastructure Consortium for Africa, 'Who Is Financing Africa's Infrastructure Development?'. Accessed 10 January 2025. https://www.icafrica.org/en/topics-programmes/who-is-financing-africa%2%80%99s-infrastructure-development/.

116 Global Alliance for Improved Nutrition, 'GAIN's Response to Covid 19 – Keeping Food Markets Working'. *Impact Story*, no. 9 (2022).

117 Erik Bruyland, *Kobalt Blues: de Ondermijning van Congo 1960–2020* (Lannoo, 2021).

118 Ibid.

119 Umicore, 'Umicore and STL Sign Partnership Related to Germanium Recycling'. Accessed 10 January 2025, https://www.umicore.com/en/news-room/umicore-and-stl-sign-partnership-related-to-germanium-recycling/.
120 McKinsey Global Institute, *Reimagining Economic Growth in Africa: Turning Diversity into Opportunity*, 16.
121 African Union, *The African Leaders' Nairobi Declaration on Climate Change and Call to Action* (Nairobi, September 2023).
122 Economist Intelligence Unit, 'Investor Interest in Kenya's Renewable Energy Sector Rises'. Accessed 10 January 2025. https://www.eiu.com/n/investor-interest-in-kenyas-renewable-energy-sector-rises/.
123 Power for All, *Powering Jobs Census 2022: The Energy Access Workforce* (September 2022), 12.

CHAPTER 4

ECONOMIC DYNAMISM
FROM THE BOTTOM UP

How can we create a better future for those working in the informal economy and in agriculture in Africa? There is certainly a role to play here for several enablers, including education, trade policy and infrastructure – the topics we have already discussed. In this next chapter, I focus on the tangible tools at our disposal for supporting the entrepreneurial spirit and drive of the many thriving informal enterprises – and that dynamism comes from the bottom up.

In the previous chapter, we saw that formal companies from industry and the service sector will not be able to quickly generate large numbers of new jobs. However, these are needed to keep pace with demographic growth in Africa.

Therefore, informal enterprises, micro-enterprises, small family agricultural enterprises complemented by small and medium-sized enterprises will be key for the African economy for a long time to come – probably three decades. Africa's economic dynamism, therefore, comes from the bottom up.

More than 80 per cent of the population in sub-Saharan Africa has no social protection whatsoever.[1] There is a link between the absence of social security and the importance of the informal economy. In fact, the lack of a social safety net is the reason many small entrepreneurs in Africa became entrepreneurs in the first place: because they were not entitled to unemployment benefits, health insurance or a pension. They became entrepreneurs out of necessity. Nonetheless, they still demonstrate a great deal of entrepreneurial spirit.

That large universe of informal enterprises and small-scale agricultural companies is therefore essential because they provide a source of income to people at the bottom of the socio-economic pyramid.

Finance for MSMEs

In the previous chapter, I pointed out the importance of informal enterprises (smallholder farmers, household enterprises and micro-enterprises) for employment. In addition, small and medium-sized enterprises (SMEs) are also crucial for employment. Many of the SMEs are also part of the informal economy. SMEs are often successfully developed micro-enterprises, and we see an uninterrupted continuum between micro-enterprises and SMEs. In the economic literature and in reports from development banks, this universe ranging from micro-enterprises to small enterprises to medium-sized enterprises is therefore increasingly referred to as the MSME sector (micro-, small and medium-sized enterprises). However, different definitions of MSMEs are also used. IFC (the investment arm of the World Bank Group) defines MSMEs in terms of number of employees, total assets and annual sales. In their definition, micro-enterprises have up to 10 employees, small enterprises up to 49 and medium-sized enterprises up to 300.[2] This definition is not really applicable to Africa. A specific report by the World Bank on 'Youth employment in Sub-Saharan Africa' uses a maximum limit of, respectively, 5 (micro-enterprises), 20 (small enterprises) and 50 (medium-sized enterprises) employees.[3] This last definition is more appropriate to the situation in Africa.

MSMEs need working capital to increase their turnover. This allows small businesses to grow and not only provide the entrepreneur with a job, but over time also become modest employers themselves. This was nicely illustrated by the story about Béatrice's sewing workshop in Rwanda. That workshop was set up using the founder's humble savings, but thanks to a loan, it was able to grow. It now employs 12 people.

About two decades ago, there were financial institutions that exclusively served micro-entrepreneurs (microfinance institutions) and other financial institutions that focused on SMEs. In 1976, Muhammad Yunus, an economics professor from Bangladesh and winner of the 2006 Nobel Peace Prize, founded the Grameen Bank, which provided modest loans to female micro-entrepreneurs. The same financing model was then replicated in many other parts of the world. Long before Yunus came along, though, Africa and other continents had the tontine system, in which a group of women took turns to lend a sum of money to other members of the group for a month. On a larger scale, too, there were (and still are) credit and savings cooperatives.[4] In the last two decades, many microfinance institutions have supplemented their existing microfinance activity with SME financing. Often these financial institutions were keeping apace with the growth of their clients. Today, the distinction between pure microfinance institutions and SME banks has become less relevant. There are many financial institutions that serve both micro-entrepreneurs and SMEs. One example is LAPO in Nigeria, which started out as a microfinance institution based on the Grameen model. Today, LAPO has become a large financial institution that still provides credit to micro-entrepreneurs, but also to SMEs. These financial institutions are now referred to as the financial inclusion sector. I will refer to these as MSME banks.

I have always found it important to meet as many small entrepreneurs and farmers as possible, as they are the customers of these MSME banks. I wanted to find out as much as possible about their living conditions, about how they make ends meet (or don't), whether or not loans help, and how they finance their children's upbringing. In recent years, I have visited and spoken to hundreds of small entrepreneurs and farmers in various countries in Africa, Asia and Latin America. In India, together with my Indian colleagues, I made a detailed reconstruction of the budget of a farming family in Uttar Pradesh. They had just one buffalo and were taking out a loan to buy a second buffalo. This analysis was later used in training courses provided by MSME banks. I have also met numerous women's groups who take out a so-called solidarity group loan with an MSME bank. These are loans that women jointly take out and repay, without having to provide a guarantee, but where they act as guarantors for each other. These loans often do not amount to more than a few tens of euros per person. The weekly or fortnightly sessions of these groups typically start with a short introduction by the MSME bank representative, sometimes supplemented with a training session, for example, on cultivation methods or financial planning. At the end of the session, the women have to make their recurring repayment. All amounts are neatly recorded in a book.

The rich colours and smells of those encounters will stay with me forever: the slums in Lagos (Nigeria) and Nairobi (Kenya), the *cités* of Kinshasa and the Ugandan countryside. Women wearing a colourful *paan* and sitting on plastic chairs. Or on the ground amid a scented palette of charcoal and dried fish. I have so much admiration for these women: they are strong and resilient and do everything they can to provide their families with an income, especially for the sake of their children.

For many years, I was also a director of African MSME banks, first in Nigeria, then in Uganda. The Ugandan MSME bank (Finance Trust Bank) was founded by the country's women's movement, which showed great commitment to and solidarity with vulnerable women's groups. I was deeply impressed by the sessions in rural Uganda, where the bank's female CEO, an impressive character, would address large groups of women. She showed true empathy, solidarity and connection.

These MSME banks are not a silver bullet for eradicating poverty (as Muhammad Yunus himself had rather too enthusiastically declared[5]). But they are a way to finance the growth of the informal economy. They are also not a panacea. They sometimes have little or zero impact and can even do more harm than good (as illustrated by the example at the end of this section).

Having followed these banks closely over the past 20 years, I believe that in many areas they can have a positive impact. By making working capital available, they support entrepreneurs in expanding their economic activities. For example, farmers gain access to much-needed pre-financing for their harvest. In many cases, these loans act as a catalyst for the growth of the company or agricultural activity. Over time, small businesses that grow can start to hire people, which is good for employment.

I have also found that MSME banks have an emancipatory effect. In Nairobi, I met Jennifer Kariuku. She was a customer of the Kenya Women Finance Bank (KWFB), a specialised MSME bank for women entrepreneurs. She had a shy but very endearing personality. Over 10 years, she had grown from a simple market seller of fabrics to a textile wholesaler with five employees. All this time, she had been a member of a women's solidarity group that took out a group loan with the KWFB. Although she had outgrown this kind of group credit and could have taken out a personal loan from the KWFB without any problem, she remained a member of the group and faithfully attended the monthly meetings. She explained to me that the group members had become her confidantes and that they had helped her become more self-confident. The human, emancipatory benefit of these kinds of groups is not to be underestimated. In 2009, Incofin invited her to its AGM in Ghent. Many of the more than two hundred attendees still remember her captivating story to this day. Incidentally, a study estimates that 58 per cent of all African MSMEs are women-owned.[6]

A recent global survey showed that access to credit had led to increased revenues for 70 per cent of MSME bank customers in sub-Saharan Africa and that more than 20 per cent of businesses had taken on additional people.[7] This indicates that MSME banks are indeed effective in terms of income generation and job creation.

More than 60 per cent of MSMEs in sub-Saharan Africa state that they do not have sufficient access to financing.[8] It is the government's responsibility to ensure that the right regulations are in place to allow the financial sector to work efficiently. Development banks and private investors can contribute to a robust financial sector by investing in financial institutions that focus on the MSME sector.

A chicken farm near Mount Kenya

Sarah Njuguna lives in Gitare (Kenya), a tiny village with a pleasant climate at an altitude of around 2,000 metres near Mount Kenya, 150 kilometres north of Nairobi. Sarah is a customer of Juhudi Kilimo, a rural MSME bank focused on lending to small farmers. Incofin is one of its shareholders. The institution has 53,000 customers, and the average customer loan is €300. When I visited Sarah, she and her husband had 1,300 laying hens. They sold the chicken eggs directly to hotels in Nairobi, and Sarah's husband transported them in his own van. They also had three cows, a calf and a goat, and grew corn, rice and cabbage.

Their first loan was €500 and their most recent was €2,500 – this was used to expand the battery cage. Sarah's next plan was to take out a loan to build a mechanical well. They already had a well, but Sarah had to operate it manually. The well was 50 metres deep, and she was using a 50-litre barrel to hoist the water up. I tried it myself, and it took a lot of muscle to bring up the barrel when it was full of water. Sarah was a smiley, optimistic woman, even though the family led a very simple lifestyle.

Feeling the heat of the financial crisis

From 2007–2010, the MSME banking sector came under great pressure. The bankruptcy of Lehman Brothers rocked the global economy, and the financial crisis seeped into the Global South. This also caused problems for local entrepreneurs.

This was the case for livestock farmers in Nicaragua, for example, who traditionally export their meat to the United States. The recession meant that American consumers were buying less meat, causing meat prices to plummet. The small livestock farmers in Nicaragua were no longer able to sell their meat or only at far below market rate. This reduced the income of small farmers from Nicaragua, who were in turn no longer able to repay their loans. Numerous Nicaraguan MSME banks ran into problems. On top of that, the populist Sandinista president Daniel Ortega announced – out of political opportunism – that entrepreneurs no longer had to repay their loans. These statements fuelled the 'no-pago' movement,[9] which pushed the entire sector into a deep crisis. The country's largest MSME bank even went bankrupt.

In India, the sector also faced major problems due to a combination of a stagnant economy and the excessive debts of Indian MSMEs. These problems were caused by an aggressive commercial policy by MSME banks, which – in pursuit of profit – had pushed loans down the throats of their customers, far beyond their ability to repay them. In addition, some Indian banks used irresponsible practices to force their customers to repay. Violence and imprisonment, with the active support of the police, were unavoidable. These abuses even led to suicides among micro-entrepreneurs from the state of Andhra Pradesh. The suicides received a lot of press coverage and provided grounds for political intervention, after which the banks were subjected to strict regulations, including maximum interest rates.

The 2007–2010 crisis cleaned up the sector. In its aftermath, all kinds of initiatives were taken to ensure that MSME banks operate responsibly and put the well-being of their customers first. For example, the Social Performance Task Force (SPTF)[10], which brings together more than 1,400 MSME banks worldwide, developed a set of universal principles for managing and monitoring their social mission. These include social strategy, management's involvement in this, providing appropriate services and products, customer protection, provision of good staff training, growth and profitability management, and finally respect for the environment.

In 2019, I had the privilege of becoming chairman of this organisation. The SPTF principles are used by social investors (such as Incofin) to screen MSME banks. They only invest in banks that score well and that have a positive and relevant impact on entrepreneurs. They have to ensure that MSME banks meet a number of conditions, the most important of which, in my opinion, are the following:

1. MSME banks must develop financial and non-financial services that best meet the needs of their customers and that strengthen the financial resilience and health of their customers. So it is not just about loans but also about payment services, crop insurance, health insurance, savings products, pension plans, advice or facilitating access to the market. MSME banks need to take a holistic approach and do more than just provide customers with access to cash. They must also offer a range of non-financial services.[11] They can support marginalised groups (for example, with a focus on female entrepreneurs) or help their customers with climate adaptation (for example, by financing climate-resistant crops). MSME banks play a key role in strengthening the financial resilience of their customers. In doing so, they must work in an innovative, entrepreneurial and creative way. The best way for them to identify their customers' needs

and preferences is through research and surveys, and they should develop custom products for the benefit of their customers, even though that may involve more risk or costs.

2. MSME banks must show a great sense of responsibility when granting loans, remembering that their customers are vulnerable for many reasons: they are less well educated, they have limited knowledge of financial services, the financial resilience of their company and therefore their negotiating capacity is limited, and they are exposed to numerous external risks (poor harvest, illness, etc.). Concern for the well-being and progress of their customers must be top priority. There is always a temptation for profit-hungry MSME banks to force their customers into taking the largest possible loan. More than in other economic sectors, the social mission and ethical mindset of the management team are crucial for generating a positive impact. The absence of this can lead to an MSME bank having a detrimental impact.

3. MSME banks must ensure that they grant tailor-made loans. This is only possible if they carefully analyse the financial situation of their customers and adjust the size of the loan to the specific situation of the entrepreneurs. It should be neither too small (serving no purpose) nor too big (forming a stranglehold). Not all MSMEs are able to absorb a loan. The repayment schedule of the loan (amounts, term, repayment frequency) must be adapted to the repayment capacity of the MSME. The interest rate charged must be reasonable. The loan should act as leverage for the entrepreneur's business activities, so that on balance they can increase their turnover and profitability. A loan can enable a small merchant to stock more merchandise, improve sales and achieve higher profits. But for the growth of the small business to be successful, the injection of credit must be properly calibrated, no matter how modest it is. This requires effort from the bank, but not delving into it is lazy and harmful.

4. The best MSME banks develop systems that measure and monitor the economic situation of their customers over time (outcome). Based on this, the bank can determine whether it is fulfilling its social mission. These outcomes can reveal important information, such as a lack of suitable products for certain regions or groups.

Practical experience at Adrabo in Uganda

Soon after I started working for Incofin, I came across a network of passionate German investors and business leaders who cared about the fate of Africa. I became lifelong friends with some of them, including Martin Wilde, who for years was the country director for the Konrad Adenauer Foundation in Ghana. He is married to a Ghanaian woman and knows the continent inside-out. Some of the later investors in Incofin's funds would come from Germany, thanks to his network. Martin was chairman of a German business association and had an impressive network of political and entrepreneurial contacts.

Through Martin, I was invited in 2006 by a German foundation to gain more insight by spending a week living and working with a small farming family in rural Uganda. We were sent to a village in groups of two participants. I was paired up with Arnold Vaatz, who had been a member of the Deutsche Bundestag, the German Parliament, since 1998. Arnold was vice-chairman of the CDU/CSU faction. He came from the region of Dresden (Saxony) in the former East Germany. Before the Wende (the fall of the Berlin Wall), he had – together with Angela Merkel – been politically active in the clandestine opposition to the GDR rulers. Having been prosecuted, he spent six months in jail.

The German foundation had managed to convince politicians and business leaders to spend a week in rural Ugandan villages. For several of them, that week would change their lives forever.

Arnold Vaatz and I stayed with Adrabo and his family in Busiika, a small village about a hundred kilometres north of Kampala. We slept on the floor in a small house. Adrabo was married and had three children. Also living with them were two other children from relatives who had passed away. Adrabo had a small piece of agricultural land where he grew sweet potatoes, cassava (manioc) and bananas. In the morning, we helped dig beds in the fields to then plant potatoes. The sun showed us no mercy.

As evening approached, we would go and fetch water. We filled large, heavy yellow plastic jerrycans from a manual water pump that was used by the entire village community. Food for the family was prepared outside on a wood fire under a corrugated iron roof. Arnold and I had long conversations with the family while making dinner. Adrabo was a man of few words. Over time, we understood why: he had been through some traumatic experiences. His father had been murdered by supporters of Milton Obote, the president of Uganda from 1966–1971 and 1979–1985. As a young man, Adrabo had himself spent years on the run, forced into hiding in the jungle. Two years before that, a small loan had allowed him to invest in a modest battery cage. The chicken coop was still there, but there was not a single chicken in sight. They had all succumbed to bird flu. The family had to repay the loan from an MSME bank, but the battery cage, which should have served as a source of income to help them repay the loan, was empty. To repay the loan, Adrabo's wife, a nurse, had returned to work at the nearby Bugema University dispensary, even though she already had her hands full at home, including having to take care of two additional children (whose parents had died of AIDS, we later found out). Under no circumstances did the family want to default on their loan.

Adrabo was under a lot of stress because the chicken farm did not yield the expected income that would have enabled him to repay the microloan and provide him with a somewhat comfortable income. Adrabo's wife saved the family by taking up a paid job again, but the increased workload caused her a lot of suffering. By experiencing this painful situation up close, I realised more than ever how important it is for MSME banks to thoroughly consider all the risks together with their customers in advance, including the consequences of the failure of the business project. Moreover, the MSME bank must show sufficient flexibility to support its customers in such situations, for example by waiving debts. In the absence of such an approach, microfinance risks bringing about the exact opposite of what it sets out to achieve. That is why it is important to always put the interests of the MSME bank customer first and to proceed with caution. Fortunately, these situations are more the exception than the rule, and lending to MSMEs generally does lead to positive results.

Laboratory and Source of Inspiration

The activities of MSME banks have gradually shed new light on the strength of small businesses and the informal economy. Some small businesses have become modest employers over time. The ecosystem that finances these companies has generated an enormous amount of data. This has created a laboratory, as it were, that shows that entrepreneurship at the bottom of the socio-economic pyramid works and that it can have a relevant and positive social impact. Undoubtedly, not all small entrepreneurs are successful and only a minority of them are 'born' entrepreneurs. The majority of them would probably prefer a permanent, well-paid job to the risks of self-employment. But over the last decade, the economic dynamism at the bottom of the socio-economic pyramid has increasingly provided an example and source of inspiration for new initiatives. Driven African entrepreneurs have developed economic activities with real impact. This is how companies have emerged that focus on small-scale, off-grid electricity production in rural areas, through the distribution and installation of photovoltaic panels. Thanks to the services of these small companies, families in rural areas now have a source of light, which improves their quality of life and also allows their children to study in the evening. This electricity also powers the water pumps on their fields. Other companies have emerged for the small-scale production and sale of safe drinking water. Or companies that collect, recycle and sell the enormous amount of plastic waste in the streets and rivers. And then there are the companies committed to affordable housing. These socioecological companies have all experienced enormous growth in the last decade.

Impact Investments

Along with the growth of MSME banks, investment funds emerged that have attracted social investors worldwide. They saw the value in financing the MSME banking sector, even despite the risks (currency, political, default, fraud, etc.). Investment funds for MSME banks have been growing steadily over the past two decades. Over the years, social investors have also shown interest in new investment areas, for example, in financing companies in the agricultural chain. Funds have been created that invest in various socioecological companies. The collective name for investments in these kinds of activities is impact investments. This refers to investments that aim not so much at profitability, but primarily at a positive social or ecological impact and within a financially sustainable framework. The term was introduced in 2010 in a joint study by the investment bank J. P. Morgan, the Rockefeller Foundation and the Global Impact Investing Network.[12]

According to a recent survey, the total volume of impact investments (in 2024) was $1,571 billion, with investments in sub-Saharan Africa representing about a fifth.[13] The other half concerns investments in Europe and North America, for example in circular economy companies that fight food waste by selling food surpluses from restaurants and shops in a short chain.[14]

Impact investments in the South cover various sectors. The most important are renewable energy, the financial sector, agriculture and food, and health care. Other sectors include housing, water, forestry and education.

Both private investors and public development banks are involved in this. Many Western countries have a specialised, government-established investment company that focuses on impact investments in companies in developing countries. For example, the Netherlands has a long tradition of investing in developing countries through FMO (the Entrepreneurial Development Bank), which was founded in 1970 and today manages more than €6 billion.[15] Founded by Belgium in 2001, BIO Invest[16] currently manages approximately €1 billion. Germany also created a development bank out of its Kreditanstalt für Wiederaufbau (KfW), the institution established after the Second World War to carry out investments as part of the country's reconstruction through the Marshall Plan. The German government is a shareholder in KfW, the largest single-country development bank in the world, with €11 billion in outstanding investments.[17] IFC, the investment sister company of the World Bank with 189 countries as its shareholders, has more than $58 billion in investments.[18]

Private investors in impact investment funds are mainly institutional investors (pension funds, funds of funds, banks), foundations, families and individuals, mainly from Europe and the United States.

Worldwide, the contribution of private investors to impact investments is greater than that of public development banks.[19] But for impact investments in Africa, the share of public development banks is bigger than that of private investors.[20] The higher share of public investors for Africa may be due to the higher average risk profile of investments in Africa, which can deter private investors.

At Incofin, we notice that banks and fund managers, at the insistence of their customers, are showing an increasing interest in sustainable investments. More and more sustainable and ESG[21] investment funds are being set up: these invest in traditional listed companies and bonds but subject them to so-called exclusion criteria (for example: no investments in companies involved in weapons production) or require positive criteria on a social and/or ecological level. In 2019, the European Parliament commendably adopted a regulation requiring investment funds to provide detailed information on their intended ESG dimension.[22] This simplifies the search for investors looking for investments that deliver socioecological value.

Sometimes the underlying investments are not particularly sustainable. In the past, Deutsche Bank (DWS) and Goldman Sachs got into trouble with their financial regulators (German and American, respectively) for presenting their investment funds as 'sustainable' without being able to sufficiently back this up.

Impact investments go one step further and explicitly strive for a positive social or ecological impact, which is also monitored and measured. These impact investments represent only a fraction of the total universe of ESG investments, typically listed company shares and bonds. While impact investments represent $1,164 billion, sustainable investments amount to $31,000 billion.[23] This means that impact investments account for only 3.7 per cent of sustainable investments.

Why is it that these investments are still relatively underdeveloped, even though they make a genuine contribution to development? There are several reasons for this. Firstly, impact investments are not tradable investment products. Take, for example, a capital participation in an unlisted African agricultural company. The participation cannot – unlike a share in a listed company – be sold from one day to the next. This is what's known as an illiquid investment. These kinds of investments require the investor to commit their investment for a period of, say, seven years before it is made 'liquid' – i.e. sold. The question is whether, after seven years, the investor will find a buyer for their participation.

The second reason is sensitivity to fluctuations in value. The African investment in our example is exposed to numerous risks, least of all serious exchange rate fluctuations. Over the years, African currencies have generally declined in value against the euro, meaning that the investment also decreases in value. Sometimes, the government in the country of the investment announces a freeze on repayments abroad, as Incofin experienced in Nigeria and Guinea, almost wiping out our investment. In addition, political shocks in Africa often have a disastrous impact on the value of the investment. For example, in 2007, there were violent ethnic tensions in Kenya between Kikuyus, Luos and Kalenjins. These posed a threat to the physical integrity of Incofin's investments. Or arbitrary political decisions are made to the detriment of foreigners, as we experienced in Zambia. While those situations have been the exception rather than the rule, they can deter investors.

The third reason is related to European regulations. Europe starts from the principle of protecting the interests of European investors, a position that was bolstered after the 2008 financial crisis. Investment products that are exposed to excessive risks are not allowed to be distributed to the general public. The European regulator makes it virtually impossible to offer impact investments to a wide audience. In general, the investor in these investments must prove that they are a well-informed, professional investor and can invest a minimum ticket of €250,000. Typically, impact investments are only accessible to a very wealthy segment of the population, unless through cooperative funds.

Working towards better regulations

My German friend, Martin Wilde, and I once visited the interior of Nigeria, together with the former chairman of the Committee on Economic Cooperation and Development of the German Parliament. We had received an invitation from a socially committed Catholic priest from Enugu State. During the military regime, he had regularly come into conflict with the government and had spent some time in prison. He wanted to develop an MSME bank and needed our advice. During that trip, Martin and I brainstormed about how we could channel more private capital into investments in the Global South, especially since public budgets would never be able to meet the astronomical need. I told him about Europe's fund regulations preventing investment funds for MSME banks from being offered to the general public (except through cooperatives, which, however, have numerous restrictions). Together, we started writing a text about how German legislation (the Kapitalanlagegesetzbuch) should be amended to offer these funds to retail investors. Martin started tapping into his network. Numerous meetings and hearings with the political groups in the German Parliament followed. But in the end, we achieved our goal: the German law was amended. Incofin became an adviser for the very first German retail investment fund for MSME banks, founded by the charismatic Edda Schröder from Invest in Visions in Frankfurt.

Sustainable development goals in the South

I am convinced that impact investments can contribute to solving the numerous challenges facing our planet. It is highly doubtful whether government budgets alone will be enough to tackle all these challenges. During a historic summit in New York in September 2015, the United Nations adopted the 17 Sustainable Development Goals (SDGs) of the 2030 Agenda for Sustainable Development.

These 17 SDGs aim to mobilise the world community to, for example, end poverty, tackle inequality and combat climate change. In turn, the SDGs are essential for stability and peace in the world. They apply to both industrialised countries and the Global South, but it goes without saying that the gap between the current situation and the SDGs in the Global South is far greater.

The United Nations calculated that – in order to achieve the SDGs by 2030 – investments (by public and private investors) in the Global South must increase by $4,000 billion annually.[24] The private sector plays an essential role in closing that gap.[25] With this in mind, I find it incomprehensible that Europe is not making a bigger effort to adjust investment fund regulations. I cannot understand why people who want to consciously invest in impact still have to overcome all kinds of hurdles.

As an aside, it is worth noting that impact investments are especially popular among millennials. Research shows that 61 per cent of millennials are interested in this. Among the baby boomers and older generations, only 23 per cent are interested. And more than half of investment advisers under the age of 40 display a personal interest in impact investing: a trend that gives us hope for the future.[26]

Every year, the UNCTAD monitors the evolution of SDG-related investments in the Global South. Taking into account all countries involved, in 2023 SDG-related investments amounted to $200 billion.[27] These figures don't come anywhere close to the previously stated target of $4,000 billion per year. In conclusion, the UNCTAD believes that the SDG commitments need to be urgently renewed, as 2030 is not far away.

The impact of fair trade

Since the 1980s and 1990s, numerous social initiatives have emerged where the informal economy in the South, including in Africa, is embedded in structures. For example, fair trade farmers' cooperatives have been founded, in which small farmers join forces and together achieve sufficient scale to sell their products (for example, coffee or cocoa) on the international market. They come together under the Fairtrade International umbrella organisation. Fairtrade cooperatives have become a relevant player on the global market. At the end of 2021, there were 1,930 fair trade cooperatives worldwide, bringing together 1.8 million small farmers. About a third of these are in Africa.[28]

The Fairtrade Access Fund[29] is the result of a partnership between Fairtrade International, Incofin and several impact investors, including the public development banks from Germany, Belgium and the Netherlands, a facility of the European Commission and private investors. The fund invests in 71 different companies, mainly farmer cooperatives. Through these investments, the fund supports 425,000 small farmers in Latin America and Africa who have an average of only 3 hectares of agricultural land. In Africa, the fund invests in Burkina Faso, Ivory Coast, Benin, Congo, Uganda, Kenya, Tanzania and Rwanda. The crops financed include coffee, cocoa, cashew nuts, macadamia nuts, avocado and mango.

Impact investments are only worthy of the name when the investor or initiator explicitly determines the positive social or ecological impact objective of the investment in advance and then measures and monitors it. Before investing, a so-called impact thesis or theory of change needs to be defined: What (measurable) impact is this particular investment aiming for?

The investments of Incofin's Fairtrade Access Fund are a good example of this. Loans from the Fairtrade Access Fund to fair trade-certified farmer cooperatives enable them to buy their members' harvest (for example, coffee) at a guaranteed price and sell it on the world market. This means that, at the start of the season, farmers can count on a predetermined revenue. With each new loan, the fund tries to estimate in advance what the impact will be. Investments are considered based on maximum impact. The Fairtrade Access Fund measures how many farmers will use the system and what their additional income will be. The fund also maintains data on the size and productivity of farmers' agricultural land.

The Fairtrade Access Fund also provides long-term loans to farmer cooperatives, for example, to replace old, less productive coffee plants or to plant new varieties that are better able to withstand changing climate conditions. With a coffee plant taking four or five years to bear fruit, the loans help the farmer bridge this long investment period. The fund also monitors the production levels of cooperatives with new coffee plants.

Lessons Learnt

What lessons have I learnt from more than twenty years of experience with impact investing in Africa? What has worked and what has not? And why?

Let me first touch on the regional allocation of our investment portfolio. Incofin invests not only in Africa, but also in Latin America and Asia. Over the last 20 years, the share of African investments has fluctuated between 10 and 20 per cent of our total investment portfolio. Latin America and Asia have generally been allocated a larger share of the portfolio. We saw earlier that extreme poverty in Africa is higher in both relative and absolute terms compared to other continents. Had we based the regional allocation of the portfolio on the poverty level of each continent, we would probably have invested more in Africa. The fact that we didn't is because our investments in Africa were exposed to comparatively greater risks than in other continents. This prompted our Investment Committee to be more cautious about investments in Africa.

First of all, the exchange rate risk mentioned earlier weighs more heavily in Africa than elsewhere. To illustrate: in 2014, you got €46 for 10,000 Nigerian Naira. Ten years later, you got only €5.6 for the same 10,000 Naira, or just 12 per cent of the original value. Sometimes investments could be hedged against exchange rate risk (this was the case for fixed-term loans). But the cost of hedging was so high that the investment made a loss. For long-term capital participation, exchange rate hedging is not an option. As a result, we invested less in African countries with a high risk of currency devaluation. If this risk were to be borne by a third party (for example, a European government agency), more impact investments would find their way to Africa. In 2024, Incofin set up a new investment fund that invests exclusively in African food companies for domestic markets. The government investors in this fund agreed to absorb part of the fund's exchange rate losses. This allowed the fund to protect itself from the exchange rate risk and play its role as an investor in and catalyst for food companies to the full.

The risk of exposure to arbitrary government measures was another sore point. MSME banks are of course subject to monitoring by the financial authorities in all countries. It is important that this monitoring is fair, balanced and neutral. But this was not always the case. A capital participation by Incofin in a Zambian MSME bank was almost lost after the central bank imposed unreasonably high capital requirements that targeted only foreign investors. Incidents like this did not exactly help us invest more in Africa.

Our African investments were also subject to political risks. Our loans to agricultural cooperatives in eastern Congo ran into problems due to the ongoing unrest in the region. However, we also experienced the ripple effect of political turbulence in other parts of the world: for example, after the military takeover in Myanmar or during the protest movements in Nicaragua. The political risk in Africa is not necessarily greater than in Asia or Latin America. However, from the outset we avoided war zones such as Sudan or unstable regions such as Mali.

The same applies to fraud cases. Although we have had some fraud cases in Africa, they were no more frequent than those elsewhere.

On the positive side, there are a multitude of investment opportunities. We receive investment requests from Africa almost daily, too many to respond to. From these, we have always been able to distil the requests with potential. These are investment opportunities with a proven track record, a well-thought-out business plan and, above all, capable management with ambitious goals to deliver social impact. One example is the MSME Finance Trust Bank in Uganda. This institution grew out of the Ugandan women's movement Uganda Women Trust, founded in 1984. Over time, the organisation developed from a credit fund for women to a fully fledged bank. The bank, whose motto is 'putting women first', provides services that specifically target women, such as savings accounts with favourable terms linked to health insurance or long-term loans for female entrepreneurs. Finance Trust Bank is led by the charismatic CEO Annet Nakawunde Mulindwa. Rarely have I seen such a driven leader. Another example is the previously mentioned macadamia nut cooperatives in

Kenya: these enterprises are led by teams that combine strong business and commercial insight with social drive. I have always found it a privilege to be able to meet such entrepreneurs.

However, I see room for African companies to invest more in technology and digitalisation, especially when I compare them with their peers in India. Incofin has invested heavily in Indian impact enterprises. This gave me the opportunity to compare African companies with similar companies in other parts of the world. During my visits to Indian companies (both financial institutions and agri-food companies), I was struck by how much their operations have been digitalised. For example, I saw how the production and logistics chain of the agricultural companies I visited were managed very efficiently thanks to digital processes. Although Africa is a breeding ground for technological enterprises, technology is still not gaining enough ground in traditional sectors. There is still work to be done here. A way to share experiences between African and Indian companies could prove fruitful.

Africa has a vibrant economic dynamism that is coming from the bottom up. It is not the governments or large conglomerates driving the economy, but a huge universe of businesses and MSMEs that provide millions of Africans with a job and an income. Their dynamism plays an essential role in absorbing the influx of young people into the labour market.

We also found that the successful financing of enterprises and MSMEs has strengthened this dynamism and inspired Africans to start up lots of other socially conscious entrepreneurial initiatives.

Global impact investments play a prominent role in financing, developing and supporting these kinds of initiatives. So their importance is not to be underestimated. Every effort must, therefore, be made to channel as much capital as possible into these funds, from both public development banks and private investors. Impact investments represent an essential shift for the future of Africa.

There are still significant obstacles to the further growth of these investments, not least due to restrictive regulations regarding the distribution of these funds to the public. However, impact investments offer every citizen the opportunity to invest in sustainability and support employment in Africa. Governments should not only show a legitimate concern to protect the investor from risk but also support the distribution of impact investments with appropriate regulation. These funds are part of a new, sustainable view of the economy, which is much more focused on people and respect for the planet.

Notes

1 UNDP and ILO, *Informality and Social Protection in African Countries: A Forward-looking Assessment of Contributory Schemes* (New York, 2021), 16.

2 International Finance Corporation, 'Definitions of Targeted Sectors'. Accessed 10 January 2025. https://www.ifc.org/en/what-we-do/sector-expertise/financial-institutions/definitions-of-targeted-sectors.

3 Deon Filmer and Louise Fox, 'Youth Employment in Sub-Saharan Africa'. Africa Development Series (World Bank, 2014), 156. doi:10.1596/978-1-4648-0107-5.

4 Yves Fournier and Alpha Ouedraogo, 'Les coopératives d'épargne et de crédit en Afrique: Historique et évolutions récentes'. *Revue Tiers Monde,* Vol. 37, No. 145, 1996, 67–83.

5 *The Guardian,* 'The Nobel Prize Winner Who Wanted to Make Poverty a Museum Piece', 13 October 2006.

6 European Investment Bank, *Finance in Africa: For Green, Smart and Inclusive Private Sector Development* (Luxembourg, 2021), 21.

7 Sasha Dichter, Delvin Olmack, Elloe Rodgers, and Akanksha Singh, *60 Decibels Microfinance Index* (2022), 40–44.

8 European Investment Bank, *Finance in Africa: for Green, Smart and Inclusive Private Sector Development* (Luxembourg, 2021), 16.

9 'No pago' is Spanish for 'I'm not paying'.

10 Social Performance Task Force. Accessed 10 January 2025, https://sptf.info/.

11 Kusisami Hornberger, *Scaling Impact: Finance and Investment for a Better World* (Washington, DC, 2023), 40.

12 Global Impact Investing Network, J. P. Morgan, and The Rockefeller Foundation, 'Impact Investments: An Emerging Asset Class'. *Global Research,* 29 November 2010.

13 Global Impact Investing Network, *Sizing the Impact Investing Market 2024* (New York, 2024), 2.

14 For example: Too Good To Go. Accessed 11 January 2025. https://www.toogoodtogo.com/en-gb.

15 FMO – Dutch Entrepreneurial Development Bank. Accessed 11 January 2025. https://www.fmo.nl/.

16 Belgian Investment Company for Developing Countries (BIO), 'About BIO'. Accessed 11 January 2025. https://www.bio-invest.be/en/about-bio.

17 KfW, 'Reporting 2023'. *About KfW.* Accessed 11 January 2025. https://www.kfw.de/About-KfW/Reporting-Portal/Reporting-2023/.

18 IFC, *Management's Discussion and Analysis and Consolidated Financial Statements* (30 June 2024).

19 D. Hand, M. Ulanow, H. Pan, and K. Xiao, 'Sizing the Impact Investing Market 2024'. *The Global Impact Investing Network* (GIIN, 2024), 5.

20 OECD, *Social Impact Investment 2019 – The Impact Imperative for Sustainable Development* (OECD Publishing, 2019), 103.

21 ESG stands for Environmental, Social, and Governance.

22 Regulation (EU) 2019/2088 of the European Parliament and of the Council of 27 November 2019 on sustainability-related disclosures in the financial services sector, *Official Journal of the European Union L* 317 (9 December 2019), 1–16. Usually called the SFDR (Sustainable Finance Disclosure Regulation).

23 Symbiotics and Swiss State Secretariat for Economic Affairs SECO, 'Private Asset Impact Fund Report 2020' (2020), 15.
24 United Nations, Inter-agency Task Force on Financing for Development, *Financing for Sustainable Development Report 2024: Financing for Development at a Crossroads.* (United Nations, 2024), 2. https://developmentfinance.un.org/fsdr2024.
25 Ibid., 68–91.
26 Hornberger, *Scaling Impact: Finance and Investment for a Better World*, 139.
27 United Nations Conference on Trade and Development (UNCTAD), *World Investment Report 2024*, 30.
28 Fairtrade International, 'Overview'. Accessed 11 January 2025. https://www.fairtrade.net/impact/overview.
29 Incofin Fairtrade Access Fund, 'Mission'. Accessed 11 January 2025. https://incofinfaf.com/#mission.

CHAPTER 5

HOW IS EUROPE CONTRIBUTING TO MORE JOBS IN AFRICA?

In the final chapter, I look at the position and role of Europe: Can the EU contribute to more employment in Africa and, in doing so, create more prosperity by 2050?

First, I look at whether and how European development cooperation is the answer to the major challenges from the first chapter. I then turn my attention to the changes in European-African relations and to the possible consequences of this new European approach. Based on my own experience with European policy mechanisms, I try to formulate specific recommendations. Finally, I consider the Chinese presence in Africa, which at the moment is seriously challenging the European approach.

Is Development Cooperation the Answer?

In the previous chapters, we saw that to keep pace with demographic growth, job creation is of the utmost importance: that observation is at the core of my vision for the future of Africa. More jobs are essential for generating the much-needed prosperity.

Is development cooperation the answer to this? But before we answer that, what exactly is development cooperation? There is actually no definition for the term.[1] It is primarily about support for the Global South through various channels: donations, loans, budget support, investments, humanitarian aid, support in areas such as health and education, technical assistance and recently also military assistance. Strangely enough, the term refers to the activity of the donor, not of the recipient.

Development cooperation is sometimes divided into pillars. The first pillar refers to official bilateral development cooperation between countries, for example, between Belgium and Congo. The second pillar is about multilateral development cooperation by international players such as the World Bank or the EU. The third pillar is development cooperation by non-governmental organisations (NGOs). The fourth pillar refers to a range of private initiatives in society at large. In this chapter, I will mainly focus on the official development cooperation covered by the second pillar and particularly by the EU.[2]

The African development economist Carlos Lopes, quoted earlier, is opposed in principle to official development cooperation, because it makes African governments donor-dependent and does not give them the responsibility required to address the true needs of their countries.[3] According to Lopes, the importance of Official Development Assistance (ODA) is very relative. In 2023, $59 billion in ODA flowed from the rest of the world to sub-Saharan Africa.[4] In the same year, money transfers from emigrated Africans to their families in their countries of origin (the remittances) in sub-Saharan Africa amounted to $54 billion, so almost the same amount. He also believes that African governments are too preoccupied with discussions about the use of development aid and not enough with pursuing a policy with mechanisms over which they have total control.

According to the Zambian economist Dambisa Moyo, the decades-long financing flows to Africa did not make any difference. She shows that, over a period of three decades, most donor-dependent African countries even recorded negative growth of an average of 0.2 per cent per year.[5] She believes that this is because ODA undermines the empowerment of African leaders and also promotes corruption. For example, 25 per cent of all funds allocated to Africa by the World Bank are said to have been misappropriated.[6]

In 2006, American professor and former adviser to the World Bank William Easterly published the controversial *White Man's Burden*, in which he severely criticises ODA.[7] Easterly targets the Planners: development agencies that draw up and impose development agendas and plans from the top down, with little knowledge of (or interest in) the reality on the ground. These plans are doomed to failure. On top of that, they are impractical and out of touch.

Easterly makes a plea for the Searchers: people who are willing to listen to the poor, to learn, and in doing so, make progress. He refers to smaller NGOs that are well placed to succeed because they know the reality on the ground and because they pursue a limited number of well-defined and realistic objectives, such as promoting education or easier access to drinking water in a particular region.

Developing countries perform best when they take their future into their own hands and reduce their dependence on donors. Botswana is – again – an example of this: the country has grown by 6 per cent annually between 1960

and today. Development cooperation with Botswana has since almost completely been phased out.[8]

Lopes, Moyo and Easterly all question the top-down model of development aid because it takes responsibility away from these countries. It does not
stimulate enough ownership. However, this is crucial, both on a micro and
macro level.

Stefan Dercon adds another dimension. According to him, it is unfair to
say that aid is wasted. 'Nevertheless, critics are right that the overall record is
typically not so impressive when assessing the overall impact on growth and
development of aid spending in the last five decades across all developing countries. [...] In countries with a development bargain and thus a commitment
by those with the power to pursue growth and development, aid may well be
used effectively over time, so long as it is provided in ways consistent with the
country's own plans and elite deals.'[9]

Fortunately, change is underway. The 2005 Paris Declaration on Aid
Effectiveness, signed by more than a hundred countries and multilateral development agencies, marked a turning point: the signatories agreed to replace
the old donor-recipient model with a new partnership model, based on the
principles of ownership, alignment, harmonisation, managing for results, and
mutual accountability.[10] The new approach was supposed to give people and
communities a voice so they could take real ownership. Organisations on the
ground were encouraged to increasingly move away from top-down planning and towards partnerships based on dialogue and co-creation with local
organisations. The declaration was further finetuned in subsequent conferences (such as the Busan Partnership for Effective Development Co-operation
of 2011). The question is, of course, whether these wonderful principles were
put into practice. The OECD developed a methodology to assess the quality
of partnering and how high-level principles were applied. It was called the
Global Partnership monitoring exercise. A very extensive monitoring exercise
took place in 2018.[11] Taking part in this exercise were 86 countries, including
40 from Africa. The results were mixed. On the positive side, an observation was made that partner country governments (developing countries) had
made significant progress in strengthening national development planning.
The proportion of partner countries with a high-quality national development
strategy had almost doubled from 36 per cent in 2011 to 64 per cent in 2018.
However, one of the negative points was that the forward visibility of development cooperation had weakened, leaving developing countries more uncertain
about future support. Partner country governments had forward visibility and
could start medium-term planning on only 56 per cent of the development

cooperation funding they expected to receive from their development partners (developed countries) three years in advance.

And in Europe?

The 1957 Treaty of Rome establishing the European Economic Community (later the EU) came about at a time when most young African states were gaining their independence. From the outset, it provided for the establishment of a European Development Fund (EDF) to provide technical and financial assistance to African countries that some member states had ties with. After all, Europe placed great importance on the continuation of its relations with the (former) colonies. The EDF was presented as a generous gesture from Europe. However, it does raise the question as to whether this 'development policy' was not just a continuation of the colonisation project.

In the following decades, the approach to European development cooperation evolved considerably. Important pivotal moments in the cooperation with Africa were the agreements of Yaoundé (1963), Lomé (four agreements starting from 1975), Cotonou (from 2000) and Post-Cotonou or Samoa (from 2023).

The consecutive agreements between the EU (and its predecessors) and the group of countries known today as the Organisation of African, Caribbean and Pacific States or OACPS (initially founded in 1975 as part of the Georgetown Agreement) cover a period of 60 years and express the changing vision of international cooperation. In a fascinating paper, James Mackie, lecturer at the College of Europe in Bruges, analyses how the interpretation of the concept of development cooperation has evolved since the Lomé Convention of 1975.[12] The Lomé Convention dates from a period in which a significant part of the international community promoted the New International Economic Order (NIEO). The emphasis at that time was on the importance and necessity of financial transfers from the North to the Global South. The well-known objective that rich countries had to spend 0.7 per cent of their GDP on development cooperation dates from that period. The Lomé Convention encouraged developing countries to take ownership of development cooperation. EU Commissioner Claude Cheysson is quoted as having said to developing countries: 'It is your money! You should use it to meet your priorities in the best possible way.' But over the following decades, the lofty principles of the Lomé Convention gradually faded into the background. There were several reasons for this. In the 1980s, the world was facing an unprecedented debt crisis, after which the IMF rolled out its ruthless Structural Adjustment Programs, which were very detrimental to developing countries. This overshadowed all other discussions on aid and development. In the 1990s, after the fall of the Berlin Wall, the African, Caribbean and Pacific countries (ACP) were no longer the only poorer countries Europe was interested in. In the 1990s, many critical reports on development cooperation were published, including the Green Paper of the EU Commission in 1997, which criticised the European development policy of the previous decades. In that period, an international consensus was also reached around the global agenda of the Millennium Goals. These evolutions had a major impact on the content of the last agreement (the 2023 Samoa Agreement), which is very different from the Lomé Convention of 1975. The importance of development cooperation is less prominent in the Samoa Agreement. Rather, the new agreement is about a political partnership with the overall purpose 'to generate mutually beneficial outcomes on common and intersecting interests and in accordance with their shared values'. The agreement first refers to the SDGs 2030 Agenda and the climate objectives of the Paris Climate Agreement and only then to the classic objective of poverty eradication. In addition, the EU abolished the EDF and its resources were included in the general EU budget. This meant that EU funding for the ACP has fundamentally changed to become conditional on continuing EU goodwill rather than established in a multi-annual legal contract. At the same time, from 2019 onwards, due to the revision of the ACP Georgetown Agreement, the relationship with the EU became less and less of a priority for the ACP countries. The ACP have decided to pursue a new road that is no longer linked to Europe, but instead points to a future of playing their own role as an international organisation in global development processes.

Over time, there was more focus on support for businesses, the so-called private sector development. A Joint Statement by the Council, the Member States, the European Parliament and the European Commission of June 2017 on the New European Consensus on Development included an important chapter on 'Prosperity – Inclusive and sustainable growth and jobs', which considered the creation of decent jobs, particularly for women and youth, to be essential for inclusive and sustainable growth.[13] The relevant chapter recognised micro-, small and medium-sized enterprises as enablers of sustainable development and essential factors in the fight against poverty. In the statement, the EU committed to promoting broad access to financial and microfinancial services. In terms of methods, the consensus considered public and private investment as a vital driver of sustainable development. 'The EU and its Member States will take action to boost investment by combining funding for sustainable development, technical assistance to develop sustainable projects and attract investors.' The statement foresaw a role for the private sector: 'The private sector can contribute to the implementation of the 2030 Agenda. The EU and its Member States, in close coordination with the European Investment Bank, will promote the mobilisation of private resources for development while also promoting private sector accountability, in areas with significant transformation potential for sustainable development'. As explained in detail below, the EU has explicitly embraced a private sector development and investment approach since Jean-Claude Juncker became Commission president. This kind of paradigm shift in development cooperation will undoubtedly benefit job creation.[14]

A Fresh Start

In September 2018, at his last State of the Union, the then president of the European Commission, Jean-Claude Juncker, presented his plan for Africa under the title 'Africa–Europe Alliance for Sustainable Investments and Jobs'.[15] It was a pivotal moment in European development and Africa policy, because for the first time a plan was unveiled that prioritised investments and jobs over budget support (donations). According to Juncker, the plan embodied a radically new vision of the relationship between Africa and Europe. Its intention was to recalibrate the historically unbalanced relationship and become a win-win project for both parties. In his speech, Jean-Claude Juncker labelled Africa the 'twin continent': 'To speak of the future, one must speak of Africa – Europe's twin continent. Africa is the future'.[16]

Juncker's plan focused on job creation – especially for young people – by stimulating investments in companies. Job creation was therefore seen as the answer to Africa's demographic challenge. Juncker's plan also recognised the need for investment in infrastructure, especially in connectivity: 24 million Africans would have access to transport infrastructure.

A new mechanism was created for investments in companies and infrastructure: the European Fund for Sustainable Development (EFSD, later transformed into EFSD+), which had access to €5.1 billion of the European budget. That amount was intended to achieve a total investment of €50 billion through leverage. The intended multiplier was, therefore, 10 times the budget allocation used.[17] We arrive at this multiplier because, for example, the EFSD provides guarantee funds that should ultimately, through leverage, enable an investment of 10 times the budget used. To do this, the EFSD relies on banks and the capital market, among others, which can hedge their investment against risks thanks to the EFSD guarantee. The amount of €50 billion seems impressive, but the actual dent it makes in the European budget is only one-tenth of that amount.

The EFSD aimed to create ten million new jobs in five years, that is, two million jobs per year. With more than 20 million new young African job seekers entering the labour market every year, more needs to be done to solve the problem. Later, the EFSD halved its job creation target to five million jobs.[18]

The EU's development cooperation is structured through a seven-year cycle, which, in short, includes successive steps of budgeting, policy definition, programming, consultation with beneficiary countries, funding, monitoring and evaluation. The present cycle runs from 2021 until 2027. The previous cycle covered the period 2014–2020. Juncker's plan was announced in 2018, close to the end of the previous cycle. Its implementation interfered with the procedural mechanisms of the cycle. The merit of the plan was that it strongly emphasised the importance of a new relationship with Africa, the urgent need for job creation and the use of new financial mechanisms. This being said, these elements were already included in the 2017 Consensus, but they were given extra political attention.

On her first official trip abroad in January 2020, Ursula von der Leyen, Jean-Claude Juncker's successor, visited Ethiopia.[19] This indicated that the new Commission president also wanted to highlight the importance of European-African relations during her term of office. As early as March 2020, she presented a plan for a Comprehensive Strategy with Africa.[20] This proposed a new partnership in five areas: in addition to growth and jobs, also energy transition, digital transformation, peace and good governance, migration and mobility. The plan was the run-up to the sixth summit of the African Union and the EU.

The Covid pandemic then put the need for new debt cancellation for African countries at the top of the international agenda. The health crisis had increased public debt in sub-Saharan African countries to alarming proportions. Countries in the region were paying up to a third of their tax revenues in interest.[21] In April 2020, the IMF and the World Bank wrote off some of the debts of the poorest countries. Later that year, the G20 granted them a temporary extension, not a waiver.[22] African countries remained saddled with sky-high debts – mainly Chinese – and with the loans provided to them by private banks. I will return to the topic of Africa's debt position later.

The sixth summit of the African Union and the European Union (AU–EU) was originally planned for 2020, but – due to the Covid pandemic – ended up taking place in February 2022, a week before Russia's invasion of Ukraine.

After that, the world's attention was very much focused on the Ukrainian war. In addition to the announcement of the delivery of 450 million Covid vaccines for Africa, the final statement mentioned a €150 billion European investment package for Africa. The Africa–Europe Investment Package is part of the Global Gateway Investment Package, an even bigger package of €300 billion for investment initiatives in Asia, the Western Balkans, the Eastern Partnership (Armenia, Azerbaijan, Georgia, the Republic of Moldova and Ukraine), the Southern Neighbourhood (10 countries from the Maghreb and the Middle East) and Africa. The package applies to the period 2021–2027 and is well integrated into the seven-year budgeting cycle.

Europe hoped to include the word 'alliance' in the final declaration of the African–Europe summit in February 2022. But the African Union refused because it did not want to jeopardise its good relations with China.

The Global Gateway represents a huge budget. However, the impressive amount is the result of the requalification of existing budgets, consolidation with the budgets of the Development Finance Institutions of member states and the leverage effect. The budget of €300 billion comprises €18 billion in grants from the EU, €135 billion of investments mobilised through EFSD+ (guarantees) and €145 billion by EU Development Finance Institutions.[23] Half of this budget is allocated to the Africa–Europe Investment Package, of which a substantial amount is the result of leverage and the budgets of Development Finance Institutions. In the European budget, we find an amount of €29 billion over the period 2021–2027 for the Global Gateway in sub-Saharan Africa, quite a bit lower than the €150 billion the Commission showed off at the Africa–Europe summit, but still impressive.[24]

The first deliverable of Global Gateway is the Africa–Europe Investment Package, concentrating on sustainable investments in infrastructure (digital, energy, transport), health, education and skills, as well as climate change and environment. It aims to boost public and private investment to create sustainable growth and jobs for Africa's growing youth population. It has the overarching objective of bolstering Africa's socio-economic, green and digital transformation through innovative sources of funding. It pays particular attention to upholding high standards to create enabling regulatory frameworks. Most of these priorities had already been agreed upon between the EU and the African Union in the Joint Africa EU Strategic Partnership during the 2007 Lisbon Summit. The flagship projects of the Global Gateway include the construction of 'strategic corridors' such as from Abidjan (Ivory Coast) to Lagos (Nigeria), from Djibouti to Dar es Salaam (Tanzania) or from Cairo (Egypt) to Kampala (Uganda). The purpose of these corridors is to 'support quality connectivity infrastructure for smart, fair and affordable mobility and trade within Africa and between Africa and Europe. The Global Gateway Africa–Europe Investment Package supports the creation of transport corridors and value chains that can benefit industries in both Africa and Europe'. The Lobito Corridor between copper and cobalt mining areas in DRC and Zambia and the Atlantic Port of Lobito in Angola is one of the flagship projects that attracts most attention. It is funded by the EU, the United States, the Africa Finance Corporation (AFC) and the African Development Bank (AfDB), in partnerships with Angola, DRC and Zambia. It includes transport infrastructure investments and investments in agriculture value chains, energy, logistics and training along the Corridor. The project is still in its preparation phase. Its goals are to enhance EU access to critical raw materials. According to observers, the 'flagship project is also strategic in the sense that it seeks to embody the EU's comprehensive and cooperative approach to bolstering critical raw materials value chains. [...] Yet, effectively realizing the development opportunities will be key for the credibility of the Global Gateway and Team Europe approach, in partnership with international and local actors, and to demonstrate that is not a mere mercantilist approach of the EU to securing critical raw materials at the cost of development aid.'[25]

The Global Gateway (GG) is an ambitious initiative that indicates a renewed interest in Africa. In addition, the GG's merit is that it brings together all relevant parties in an overarching approach, involving all relevant Directorates-General and agencies, the European Investment Bank, and Development Finance Institutions of the EU member states. The GG is a major step-up in the reorganisation and coordination of the EU's policy towards Africa. As the GG represents a big change of course of the European vessel, it will take time before it is smooth sailing.

The GG approach and projects also raise some reservations. Firstly, it is not clear from the outside how the priorities of the GG are being determined, both at country level and for sub-Saharan Africa as a whole. Or how it relates to Agenda 2063, the ambitious list of priorities of the African Union for transforming Africa into the global powerhouse of the future.[26] Although the EU conducts in-depth exchanges with individual beneficiary countries as part of the seven-year EU budget cycle, resulting in a detailed Multi-annual Indicative Programme (MIP), the path from the MIP to the GG is opaque. We might also wonder how the arbitration between countries is being organised: Why does country X benefit more from the GG than country Y? And how is the African Union involved in the budget allocation? A diplomat told me that during the February 2022 summit in Brussels, African governments were unhappy about the fact that they were barely allowed to provide any input in terms of the content of the package. According to the diplomat involved, this was because the European Commission had to reach prior agreement with 27 member states, the European Council and the European Parliament. That balance is so fragile that it leaves no room for discussion with the African governments. The diplomat was very sceptical about Europe being able to approach this in any other way, because the European decision-making process is a permanent balancing act.

Secondly, the link between the projects and the EU's fundamental priorities (eradication of poverty and job creation) is diffuse. Even worse, many projects seem to instead focus on Europe's own interest in securing supplies of renewable energy and critical raw materials.[27] The intent of development cooperation can range from pure altruism to pursuing a common interest to ultimately only pursuing one's own interests. Is there a tendency to move away from altruism and even from mutual interest to prioritising European interests? Of the 225 projects on the European Commission's list of flagship projects for the period 2023–2024, 110 are on climate and energy (49 per cent), 49 on transport (22 per cent), 29 on digital (per cent), 21 on health (9 per cent) and 16 on education and research (7 per cent).[28] We might wonder how this list reflects the urgency of employment creation and poverty eradication. The GG does not include quantitative objectives for job creation, despite it being a crucial success factor.

Thirdly, notwithstanding the extensive consultations leading to MIPs, many local NGOs and social entrepreneurs on the ground are voicing their disappointment about not being heard. Can the Commission not invite those involved to develop proposals together? This could lead to the definition of some very relevant projects. For example, in eastern Congo, there is an urgent demand for initiatives that could improve access to finance for coffee and cocoa cooperatives, enabling them to export their produce. These kinds of initiatives do not require a lot of capital, but they must be carefully prepared, capitalising on local knowledge.

Finally, the pooling of efforts between the EU and the European Development Finance Institutions into Team Europe is a logical step toward achieving better coordination between European public agencies involved in Africa. At the same time, the design makes it almost impossible for outsiders to take any leading or even co-developing role in the conceptualisation of GG projects.

Cockpitism in practice

Development agencies and public development banks employ a lot of committed leaders and professional staff. Despite this, I have often been amazed at how they regularly use a top-down approach when designing their programmes and activities. From their offices in the capitals of Europe – the cockpit – they design programmes that barely take into account the situation on the ground. Some programmes are also designed solely because they are politically 'useful'. This is, for example, the case in the twilight zone between European external border control and development cooperation.

I am convinced that programmes only have a positive impact when they are created based on hands-on experience and collaboration with those involved and out of a genuine desire to have a positive impact on Africa.

I have personally witnessed several situations that revealed a lack of sound knowledge of the situation on the ground. One time was a heated discussion I had with a government investor during negotiations about a fund that would mainly finance rural MSME banks. The fund would reach about two million small farmers through investments in a dozen MSME banks. The reality of small African farmers cannot be compared with the situation of European farmers, not even small European farmers. Chicken runs on small African farms do not have ventilation. African farmers do not check whether they are respecting the European standards on maximum density of chickens in the run (in terms of kg/m^2). They don't keep statistics on this. Unfortunately, the transport of animals often takes place under dire conditions. Cows are sometimes loaded into an open lorry and their horns are tied to the sides of the lorry with ropes. I never get a good feeling when I'm confronted with this kind of abuse. The government investor was expecting the small African farmers to follow European legislation. He was rightly concerned about the environment and animal welfare. I am also a great supporter of a strict environmental policy and animal welfare, so I shared his concern. But I had a battle on my hands trying to convince him that he needed to have realistic expectations. I suggested that, as a benchmark, African farmers should use their own country's environmental standards, not the European standards. It seemed almost neo-colonialist to tell African farmers that European standards were superior to their own laws.

Thankfully, we came to a feasible solution. The man's intentions were undoubtedly good, and European environmental legislation is of course commendable, but applying it wholesale to small African farmers is a bridge too far.

I therefore argue that those responsible for government agencies should spend much more time in the field. They should not only visit African capitals or take a tour in a flashy, white, air-conditioned jeep, but also mingle with ordinary Africans in the markets and in the countryside.

The Chinese Alternative

Over the last two decades, China has left its mark on Africa through the financing and implementation of large-scale infrastructure works and through its highly visible presence in various economic sectors, including mining, construction, agriculture and food. Chinese investments have undeniably contributed to economic growth and job creation. Their approach contrasts sharply with European development cooperation, which is subject to human rights and good governance conditions. The Chinese approach is not borne out of a concern for less poverty and more jobs in Africa, but is purely inspired by economic and geopolitical self-interest.

Between 2000 and 2020, China provided 1,188 loans to African governments, totalling $159 billion.[29] More than half of the loans are intended for energy production and transport infrastructure.[30] Investments in mining account for 11 per cent.

China is a big lender for infrastructure works in Africa. For this, it uses the China Development Bank and the Export–Import Bank of China (Exim Bank), both government banks. Unlike traditional multilateral and bilateral development banks, Chinese development banks do not subject themselves to international procurement of works.[31] The result is that all Chinese-funded projects are carried out by Chinese companies (and Chinese workers). This sometimes causes bad blood among African companies, as they believe that they too have the necessary technical expertise.

China charges market-based interest rates on the vast majority of the loans it grants.[32] In more than half of the cases, the Chinese take supply contracts for natural resources (oil, copper, platinum, diamonds) as collateral. For example, a $1 billion loan to Angola was backed by oil contracts.[33]

China also often takes a pledge on the financed infrastructure, such as the construction of the port of Mombasa. As the borrower, Kenya found itself struggling to make the repayments, narrowly avoiding a seizure of the port infrastructure by the Chinese. When it came to the Mombasa–Nairobi Standard Gauge Railway (the brand new train connection between the Kenyan capital Nairobi and the port city of Mombasa), the revenue from the railway was not enough to repay the Chinese loan. In both cases, contractually Kenya could not invoke its sovereignty to avoid seizure and had to resort to other methods instead.[34] Similar transactions took place in Congo. For example, the 'contract of the century' was signed with President Joseph Kabila's Congo, granting China access to natural resources in exchange for infrastructure works. As part of the Resource for Infrastructure Agreement (2007), Chinese public companies entered into a joint venture with Congolese copper company Gécamines to manage the Dima copper mine near Kolwezi. In return, they promised to carry out $6 billion worth of infrastructure works in Congo (later reduced to $3 billion). This included the renovation of the Boulevard du 30 Juin, Kinshasa's iconic main thoroughfare. But the works were financed by a loan from China's Exim Bank to the Congolese government. Revenue from the joint venture financed the repayment of the loan. In reality, only $1.8 billion worth of infrastructure works have been carried out and no income from the joint venture has yet flowed back to the people of Congo because the revenue from the copper mine will go towards repaying the Exim Bank loan for years to come.[35] In 2021, Congolese president Félix Tshisekedi stated that he wanted to renegotiate the mining contract drawn up between his predecessor and the Chinese companies: 'It is not normal that those with whom the country has signed exploitation contracts are getting richer while our people remain poor'.[36] In May 2023, he travelled to Beijing to enter into discussions at the highest level with President Xi Jinping, based on a report from the Congolese administration that had shown the imbalance in the contract.[37]

Some have called the Chinese approach 'debt trap diplomacy': a deliberate policy by the Chinese to keep countries in a stranglehold to seize their critical infrastructure and natural resources.[38] This was the reason that Tanzania, for example, rejected the construction of the Bagamoyo port by Chinese companies. Others dispute this and point out that China has often allowed debt restructuring and is therefore open to finding solutions.[39]

Over the years, cooperation between China and Africa has intensified. In 2018, China invited African leaders to the first Forum on China–Africa Cooperation (FOCAC). This well-attended forum in Beijing takes place every three years. The initiative is part of the broader Chinese plans regarding the Belt and Road Initiative,[40] which President Xi Jinping launched in 2013.

European policymakers look on with dismay at the increasing influence of China in Africa. It is a thorn in the side of Europe, which likes to present itself as Africa's privileged partner. However, observers note that China has been treading more carefully with its new African commitments over the past five years because several countries have been unable to repay these Chinese loans.[41]

The reason for this is that the financed infrastructure projects did not generate the revenue that was expected. At the triennial Africa–China FOCAC summit in Senegal in November 2021, China announced that it would be monitoring its investments more closely. Financial commitments in Africa were reduced. The reason for this was that China was forced to accept debt restructurings.

China is also facing loan defaults in non-African countries, for example, Sri Lanka. The loans here were used to finance and build the port of Colombo in Sri Lanka. But the country ran into serious repayment problems. Nevertheless, the port was an important pillar of the Belt and Road Initiative, which appears to be losing steam.

However, during the 2024 FOCAC session in Beijing, there was renewed momentum in the relationship between China and Africa. The African leaders arrived at the conference well prepared. Many African leaders were prioritising the potential of Africa to become China's primary agricultural exporter due to its abundance of arable land and the potential for value addition in agricultural products and minerals. China met Africa's high expectations and made new financial commitments of $50 billion over a period of three years.

Weighing up the Chinese presence in Africa is very complex. On the one hand, there is criticism of the fact that China does not impose any political conditions on African policymakers, for example in the areas of human rights, fair elections and corruption. But on the other hand, some point out that China is leveraging the African economy by stimulating innovation and technology and by developing its infrastructure – all positive enablers for a structural transformation of the continent.[42]

Debt

I mentioned how the GG investment projects and Chinese infrastructure projects are usually financed by loans. Generally speaking, over the last decade, Official Development Assistance (ODA) has increasingly taken the form of loans and less and less of grants. The evolution of ODA to Africa between 2012 and 2022 shows a decrease in the grant component from 78 per cent to 70 per cent and an increase in the loan component from 21 per cent to 29 per cent.[43] China now represents 11 per cent of Africa's increasing mountain of debt.

In 2022, sub-Saharan Africa's external debt reached $833 billion.[44] The debt stock more than doubled in 10 years' time. This increase in debt is not only due to the changed composition of ODA. The debt crisis of 2008, the Covid-19 pandemic of 2020 and higher food prices after Russia's invasion of

Ukraine have also pushed up Africa's debt. In 2022, just over half of African countries had debt ratios of more than 60 per cent of their GDP, which is considered the upper limit for manageable debt.[45]

It is striking how the share of debt from private lenders has increased much faster over the years than the debt from foreign governments or multilateral institutions. Private lenders now represent 42 per cent of sub-Saharan Africa's debt. Their share of debt has quadrupled in 10 years. The fear is that African countries mainly turn to private lenders when they are desperate for financing and have no other way out. And in this scenario, private investors will charge high interest rates. In Zambia, the debate about the role of private lenders flared up in 2020 after the country defaulted on a Eurobond due to the Covid-19 pandemic. The country was facing over-indebtedness, and the high interest rates on private debt were not helping. The IMF put pressure on foreign governments and external private creditors to cancel part of Zambian debt payments between 2022 and 2025. Of Zambia's external government debt payments between 2022 and 2028, 45 per cent are to Western private lenders, 37 per cent to Chinese public and private lenders, 10 per cent to multilateral institutions and 8 per cent to other governments. Asset manager BlackRock is one of the largest holders of Zambian debt. In 2022, over 100 economists and development experts called on BlackRock and other creditors to cancel a significant amount of Zambia's debt.[46] In June 2024, an agreement on debt restructuring was reached.

Due to Africa's high-risk profile, the average interest rate on African debt is much higher than in the rest of the world. African countries pay an average of 11.6 per cent interest on a 10-year loan. Asia pays an average of 6.5 per cent, the United States 3.5 per cent and Germany 1.5 per cent.[47]

High debt levels and the resulting high-interest payments mean that seven African countries spend more on interest payments than they do on education. Furthermore, 25 African countries spend more on interest payments than on health care. The unbearable debt situation was the reason why the IMF and the World Bank provided some debt relief to the most indebted countries in April 2020, shortly after the emergence of the Covid-19 pandemic.

It is important that both the international community and private lenders agree on rules for joint debt restructuring for countries that are struggling to pay. In addition, it is important that bilateral and multilateral development banks play their full role in financing projects that contribute to the SDGs and the necessary basic economic infrastructure, so that the economies of the countries involved can grow. This is precisely what will prevent situations of over-indebtedness.

Pain Points and Future Prospects

Africa is rich in natural resources, which are indispensable for the energy transition and the fight against climate change. Economies such as China, Russia, Turkey, Qatar and Saudi Arabia are increasingly trying to gain a foothold in Africa to ensure their access to these natural resources. This explains why they are trying to curry favour with the most resource-rich African countries.

Because of its historical ties, Europe sees itself as *the* privileged partner of Africa, one step ahead of these new outsiders trying to lay their claim. However, Europe is in a different position than the newcomers. It may have the closest and longest-standing ties with Africa, but it played a questionable role in the past, not least because of its unfair appropriation of natural resources and inappropriate colonial structures. In addition, a significant part of the climate damage in Africa is due to European emissions. This last problem is not just about the past but is also the responsibility of the current generation of Europeans, even if Europe is reducing its greenhouse gas emissions.

Europe must now resolutely move on from the past and actively contribute to the restoration of the dignity of the African continent. In doing so, Europe would demonstrate how seriously it takes its fundamental values. Moreover, when driven by political ambition, it has great clout.

Since the presidency of Jean-Claude Juncker, Europe has tried to elevate its relationship with Africa. This was a good start. But much more is needed. The expectation of a privileged partner is that it is genuinely concerned about the fate of its ally, even while both parties are pursuing their own interests. A partnership presupposes a relationship based on equality and an attitude that demonstrates a willingness to listen and respect everyone's individuality and diversity. In that area, there is still a lot of work to be done. I will now go over the key pain points and obstacles.

The European approach to asylum and migration, which mainly focuses on border protection, does not demonstrate a partnership between equals. The approach is a one-sided defence with little respect for asylum seekers and migrants. Moreover, it ignores the root causes of migration, which are due, among other things, to the evolution of the African demography and the lack of opportunities for decent work. A positive policy is needed to stimulate the creation of decent work in Africa and to offer opportunities to Africans. The defensive European approach is in danger of coming back to hit it like a boomerang. In the coming decades, the European population will shrink and age. Meanwhile, Africa has the youngest population in the world. In fact, it is the only continent in the world that will see its population of youth grow over the coming decades. It would be advisable for Europe to leave more room for labour mobility in its migration policy. Labour surpluses in Africa contrast with growing labour shortages in Europe, something that is already acutely visible in the health care sector. Germany is already opening up nursing schools in Ghana and guaranteeing Ghanaian nurses work in Germany. The EU's new asylum and migration policy aims to improve labour mobility. Dutch migration experts Henk van Houtum and Leo Lucassen have made some concrete proposals on how a sustainable and just migration policy could look.

I have shown that, over the coming decades, Africa needs millions of additional jobs. Succeeding in this is crucial for African stability. Europe can respond in a targeted way with its GG Africa–Europe Investment Package. Job creation must therefore be a central objective of the ambitious European investment package. I therefore propose that the European Commission defines concrete employment objectives for its investment package, prioritises projects with a high employment impact, and develops a publicly accessible dashboard where everyone can monitor the progress of the investment package and African job creation.

The GG Africa–Europe Investment Package, represents a significant financial commitment from the EU, which is commendable. But the involvement of Africans and players on the ground remains limited. Moreover, the EU seems keen to opt for large-scale projects involving big sums of money. As a result, smaller, local but often meaningful initiatives are not being considered. I propose creating more space for on-the-ground applicants that can have real impact.

Since the need for investments in Africa is enormous, it seems obvious to not only release money from the European budget but also mobilise as much private capital as possible. The European budget is already facing a lot of challenges and – by definition – there is a limit to it. In principle, the GG is trying to attract private institutional capital in addition to budgetary resources. This is positive. At the same time, private investors are showing real interest in investments that make a positive contribution to society or the environment, also in Africa. But the European Commission is putting the brakes on making impact investments accessible to the general public. I find it paradoxical how the Commission is using public money to stimulate investments in Africa but is at the same time reluctant to create a regulatory framework for private investment funds accessible to the general public. I call on policymakers to take regulatory initiatives to allow Europeans (including private individuals) access to impact investments.

Boosting employment

I would like to remind readers how important it is for Africa to create a significant amount of (decent) new jobs. At the end of Chapter 3, I listed vectors that can contribute to significant job growth: agriculture and food processing, expanding the value chain of critical natural resources on African soil – the services industry, renewable energy production, infrastructure projects, the blue economy, creative industries, biodiversity protection activities and the huge universe of informal businesses.

Building on the analysis of the previous chapters, I now pose the question: What will give job creation in Africa a real boost? First and foremost, of course, this will come through African entrepreneurs pursuing the ambitious growth of their companies. But investors and investment funds, who provide loans to or take capital participation in African companies, are also a catalyst for jobs.

Investors in funds focused on African companies include commercial private equity funds and public Development Finance Institutions (DFIs) from both Africa and beyond. A recent study showed that nine large DFIs have invested $71.8 billion in Africa since 2010.[48] Half of this amount went to just three countries: South Africa, Nigeria and Kenya. DFIs invest mainly in financial institutions, in energy and infrastructure and in agricultural companies. DFIs are of critical importance for supporting the growth of companies and therefore deserve encouragement. However, they need to refrain from a top-down approach and must also take risks in more fragile countries.

Impact funds are also an important catalyst for jobs. Incofin's funds invest in African companies in the agro-food sector and in MSME banks, thereby accelerating their growth. The African Rivers Funds from fund manager XSML invests in SMEs in DRC, Zambia, Kenya, Angola and Uganda, a sector that previously did not initially attract the attention of investors. Investors in impact funds are investors who care about the social or ecological added value of their investments, in addition to the financial return. DFIs also invest in impact funds. Managers of private impact funds can often work more granularly in the field than DFIs (in smaller companies or in rural areas). This is the case with Incofin, for example. According to the survey mentioned above, the average investment by DFIs is between $10 million and $30 million. Incofin's average investment in Africa, on the other hand, is only $1.5 million.

Impact funds will have to multiply in the future in order to create even more jobs. This is possible, as mentioned, if Europe relaxes the regulations for these funds. In addition, Europe and the DFIs can use GG resources to support so-called Blended Finance funds: these are funds in which parties (for example, Europe, DFIs or philanthropic organisations) commit to absorbing any losses of the fund, so that the other investors have a 'cushion' and can achieve a decent return on their investment, even though the mutual investments are risky but covered. These structures act as leverage to attract catalytic capital from private investors.

It is also necessary to mobilise as many African investors as possible: African Stock Exchanges, African governments, the African Development Bank, regional development banks (such as the East African Development Bank), national development banks (such as the Development Bank of Rwanda), the previously mentioned African pension funds, the diaspora and the growing group of large African entrepreneurs (such as the Dangote Group from Nigeria).

Thanks to the presence of critical raw materials, African governments are increasingly in a position to extract maximum benefits from major foreign investment programmes such as the Belt and Road Initiative or the GG, including in the area of infrastructure. In addition, the African Union has the law on its side when it comes to demanding investment in the framework of the Climate Fund and the Loss and Damage Fund. These funds provide leverage for job creation.

Last but not least, commercial investments from outside Africa (Foreign Direct Investments, FDI) are also important for job creation: these are investments in companies on the African continent. African governments can encourage this flow of investments by ensuring a climate of legal certainty and good governance. In the last 10 years, the annual inflow of FDI amounted to between $30 billion and $70 billion.[49] Not China, but in fact European countries (UK, France, the Netherlands) are traditionally the largest FDI investors. In addition, the volume of announced greenfield projects doubled in three years to $60 billion in 2022. These projects mainly concern energy and gas supply, construction and extractive industries. They can also create additional jobs, especially when taking into account the local supply chain.

Optimising the interplay of all the investors described above can give job creation in Africa a real boost. But, as mentioned earlier, even in the most optimistic scenario, informal businesses will be essential for absorbing the influx of job seekers in the coming decades.

Notes

1 Patrick Develtere, Huib Huyse, and Jan Van Ongevalle, *International Development Cooperation Today: A Radical Shift Towards a Global Paradigm* (Leuven University Press, 2021), 32–33.

2 Ibid., 35.
3 Carlos Lopes, *How Big Is Africa?* (SOAS Century Lecture, SOAS University of London, October 2016).
4 ONE, 'Official Development Assistance'. Accessed 11 January 2025. https://data.one.org/topics/official-development-assistance/.
5 Dambisa Moyo, *Dead Aid: Why Aid Is Not Working and How There Is a Better Way for Africa* (Farrar, Strauss and Giroux, 2009), 46.
6 Ibid., 52.
7 William Easterly, *The White Man's Burden: Why the West's Efforts to Aid the Rest Have Done So Much Ill and So Little Good* (Oxford University Press, 2006). The title refers to an 1899 poem by Rudyard Kipling about the civilising mission of the West, the language of which is staggering.
8 Easterly, *The White Man's Burden*, 24–25.
9 Stefan Dercon, *Gambling on Development: Why Some Countries Win and Others Lose* (Hurst, 2022), 274–275.
10 Develtere, Huyse, and Van Ongevalle, *International Development Cooperation Today*, 88–89.
11 Organisation for Economic Co-operation and Development (OECD) and Global Partnership for Effective Development Co-operation, *Making Development Co-operation More Effective – 2019 Progress Report* (OECD, 2019).
12 James Mackie, 'Lomé to Cotonou and Beyond: What Happened to the 'Spirit of Lomé' in EU Development Cooperation?' *EU Diplomacy Paper* 07/2021 (Bruges: Department of EU International Relations and Diplomacy Studies, College of Europe, 2021).
13 Joint Statement by the Council and the Representatives of the Governments of the Member States meeting with the Council, the European Parliament and the European Commission, 'The New European Consensus on Development – Our World, Our Dignity, Our Future' (Brussels, 7 June 2017).
14 Develtere, Huyse, and Van Ongevalle, *International Development Cooperation Today*, 62–64.
15 Communication from the Commission to the European Parliament, the European Council and the Council, 'Communication on a new Africa-Europe Alliance for Sustainable Investment and Jobs: Taking Our Partnership for Investment and Jobs to the Next Level' (Brussels: COM, 12 September 2018), 643 final.
16 Develtere, Huyse, and Van Ongevalle, *International Development Cooperation Today*, 136.
17 European Commission, 'Questions and Answers – EU External Investment Plan'. Accessed 12 January 2025. https://ec.europa.eu/commission/press-corner/detail/en/memo_18_4425.
18 United Nations, 'EU External Investment Plan (EIP), Including the European Fund for Sustainable Development'. *Partnerships for the SDGs*. Accessed 12 January 2025. https://sdgs.un.org/partnerships/eu-external-investment-plan-eip-including-european-fund-sustainable-development.
19 ECDPM, 'New Year, New Aspirations for Europe-Africa Relations?'. Published 13 January 2020. Accessed 12 January 2025. https://ecdpm.org/talking-points/new-year-new-aspirations-europe-africa-relations/.

20 European Commission and High Representative of the Union for Foreign Affairs and Security Policy, *Joint Communication to the European Parliament and the Council: Towards a Comprehensive Strategy with Africa* , JOIN(2020) 4 final (Brussels, 9 March 2020).

21 Kristalina Georgieva, 'The Road Ahead for Africa—Fighting the Pandemic and Dealing with Debt' (IMF, 23 June 2021). https://www.imf.org/en/News /Articles/2021/06/23/sp062321-the-road-ahead-for-africa-fighting-the-pan-demic-and-dealing-with-debt.

22 Council of the European Union, 'Council Conclusions on International Debt Relief in Particular for African Countries', 30 November 2020. https://www .consilium.europa.eu/media/46968/st13529-en20.pdf.

23 Global Gateway, 'Global Gateway and the Private Sector'. *EU Infopoint*, 22 February 2024

24 Regulation (EU) 2021/947 of the European Parliament and of the Council of 9 June 2021 establishing the Neighbourhood, Development and International Cooperation Instrument – Global Europe, amending and repealing Decision No 466/2014/EU and repealing Regulation (EU) 2017/1601 and Council Regulation (EC, Euratom) No 480/2009, art. 6, *Official Journal of the European Union* L 209, 14 June 2021, 1–78.

25 San Bilal and Cloe Teevan, *Global Gateway, Where Now and Where to Next?*, ECDPM Discussion Paper no. 368 (Maastricht, June 2024), 11–12.

26 African Union, 'Agenda 2063'. Accessed 12 January 2025. https://au.int/en/ agenda2063.

27 Vince Chadwick, 'Scoop: Global Gateway 2024 "Flagships" Reveal EU Self-interest'. *Devex*, 26 October 2023. Accessed 12 January 2025. https://www .devex.com/news/scoop-global-gateway-2024-flagships-reveal-eu-self-interest -106447.

28 Bilal and Teevan, *Global Gateway, Where Now and Where to Next?*, 7.

29 The Boston University Global Development Policy Center, 'Chinese Loan to Africa Database'. Accessed 13 January 2025. https://chinaafricaloandata.bu .edu/.

30 B. Benkerroum, Y. Liu, P. Mabuza, and O. J. Omotilew, 'China's Infrastructure Finance in Africa: Stylized Facts and Impact of Covid 19'. African Development Bank, 2. *Africa Economic Brief*, Vol. 12, No. 8, 2021, 2.

31 Jing Gu and Richard Carey, *China's Development Finance and African Infrastructure Development. In: China-Africa and an Economic Transformation*. Edited by Arkebe Oqubay and Justin Yifu Lin (Oxford University Press, 2019), 157. DOI:10.1093/ oso/9780198830504.003.0008.

32 Benkerroum et al., 'China's Infrastructure Finance in Africa'.

33 Ibid.

34 Kanayo Umeh, 'China-backed Railway Agreement Puts Kenya's Sovereignty at Risk'. *The Guardian*, 24 August 2020. Accessed 13 January 2025. https:// guardian.ng/features/china-backed-railway-agreement-puts-kenyas-sover-eignty-at-risk/.

35 Erik Bruyland, *Kobalt Blues: de ondermijning van Congo 1960–2020* (Lannoo, 2021), 118–122.

36 Aljazeera, 'DR Congo President Seeks Review of Mining Contracts with China', 11 September 2021. Accessed 13 January 2025. https://www.aljazeera

.com/news/2021/9/11/dr-congo-leader-seeks-review-of-mining-deals-with
-china.

37 La Libre Afrique, 'La Chine et la RDC renforcent leur partenariat et discutent
    de contrats miniers', 26 May 2023. Accessed 13 January 2025. https://afrique
    .lalibre.be/77497/la-chine-et-la-rdc-renforcent-leur-partenariat-et-discutent
    -de-contrats-miniers/.

38 A statement by the Indian academic Brahma Chellaney.

39 The China Africa Research Initiative Blog, 'The Road to Who Knows Where:
    What One Highway Project in Cameroon Can Tell Us About the Complexities
    of Chinese Lending in Africa'. *China in Africa: The Real Story* (Johns Hopkins
    School of Advanced International Studies), 6 July 2021. Accessed 13 January
    2025. http://www.chinaafricarealstory.com/2021/07/the-road-to-who-knows
    -where-what-one.html.

40 Gu and Carey, *China's Development Finance and African Infrastructure Development.
    In: China-Africa and an Economic Transformation*, 148

41 The Boston University Global Development Policy Center, 'Chinese Loan to
    Africa Database'.

42 World Bank Group and China Development Bank, *Leapfrogging; the Key to
    Africa's Development? From Constraints to Investment Opportunities* (2017). Accessed
    13 January 2025. https://documents.worldbank.org/en/publication/docu-
    ments-reports/documentdetail/121581505973379739/leapfrogging-the-key-to
    -africas-development-from-constraints-to-investment-opportunities.

43 UNCTAD, 'Debt Concerns Grow as Development Aid Shifts from Grants to
    Loans', 15 April 2024. Accessed 13 January 2025. https://unctad.org/news/
    debt-concerns-grow-development-aid-shifts-grants-loans.

44 World Bank, *International Debt Report 2023* (Washington, DC: World Bank,
    2023), 53. https://doi.org/10.1596/978-1-4648-2032-8.

45 UNCTAD, 'Debt Dashboard, Regional Stories, Africa'. Accessed 13
    January 2025. https://unctad.org/publication/world-of-debt/regional-stories
    #section1.

46 Debt Justice UK, 'Open Letter to BlackRock, Zambia's Creditors and the
    G20'. Accessed 13 January 2025. https://debtjustice.org.uk/wp-content/
    uploads/2022/09/Open-letter-from-experts_09.22.pdf.

47 United Nations – UN Global Crisis Response Group, *A World of Debt: A Growing
    Burden to Global Prosperity* (July 2023), 10.

48 Africa Resilient Investment Accelerator (ARIAS), *Foundations of Growth – DFI
    Investments in Frontier Markets: Activities, Lessons Learned and Approaches to Fostering
    Investment* (June 2024), 3.

49 UNCTAD, 'World Investment Report 2024, Regional Trends Africa'.
    Accessed 13 January 2025. https://unctad.org/system/files/non-official-docu-
    ment/wir2024-regional_trends_africa_en.pdf.

CONCLUSION

The key question at the beginning of this book was: How can Africa create a future with more prosperity and less poverty for all? What answer has the research in this book provided?

The key to the solution lies in prioritising job creation. More work for everyone is the shortest route to 'redistributive growth',[1] a model in which economic growth and prosperity go hand in hand with a more equal distribution of income.

Population growth means that more young people will be looking for jobs in the coming decades. Without jobs, unemployment and migration will increase. Fortunately, the challenges that Africa faces, as described in the prosperity pentagon, also have a positive impact on employment. Thanks to its demographic evolution, Africa will have the youngest population in the world for decades to come. Today, the median age in Africa is 18. In the EU, the median age is 44: a gap of 26 years. The young African population is innovative and creative. Young Africans are developing new forms of economic activity, including in the IT sector and in the creative sectors. The ageing workforce in the rest of the world is an opportunity for more jobs for Africans.

Africa is gradually succeeding in shifting the economic centre of gravity of global value chains from outside the continent to African soil. This applies, for example, to the agri-food value chain, where raw materials are increasingly being processed in Africa. A similar dynamic is also at play in the critical raw materials sector. Africa is the main supplier of raw materials essential to the green energy transition (such as cobalt, copper and lithium). The continent is back on the geopolitical map. Foreign economic powers are putting all their resources into gaining the favour of African regimes and getting their hands on these raw materials. At the same time, this global need for raw materials and foreign interest offer African governments the opportunity to shift the balance of power in their favour. They can force foreign powers to keep a larger part of the value chain in Africa and provide more Africans with jobs. In addition, there is a huge potential for job creation in renewable energy, construction and the blue economy. Thanks to these developments, the African economy is able to offer meaningful and dignified jobs to more and more people. The first signs of an 'African Renaissance', coined by former South African president Thabo Mbeki, are starting to show.

Africans are excellent entrepreneurs who make their businesses thrive even under difficult circumstances. As an impact investor, I have met hundreds of African entrepreneurs and farmers over the past 30 years. Their inventiveness, work ethic and perseverance are phenomenal. A key conclusion of this book is that the informal sector will continue to play a major role for decades to come. This sector may not generate substantial economic growth, but it will remain an essential provider of employment.

On a social level, young people are increasingly forming activist groups to hold their political leaders accountable. The rapid dissemination of information, thanks to the mass use of mobile phones, is shaking authoritarian regimes to their core. Their shelf life has shrunk considerably, revealing the prospect of better governance.

The quality of education is crucial for the future hopes and dreams of Africa. The young population will be all the more innovative if they can rely on a good education. Africa has come a long way in improving access to education, but there is still a lot of work to be done in terms of quality. The education sector, therefore, has an important role to play in shaping a better African future.

***

During one of my visits to Guinea, I met Aboubacar Sidiki Bamba. He had previously been an undocumented immigrant in Belgium, earning a living by tending to the gardens of wealthy Brussels residents. But he had also used his time in Belgium to take computer science classes at the Université Libre de Bruxelles (ULB), without ever being enrolled there. Aboubacar was really smart. He built up a network of sympathisers in Belgium, who donated second-hand computers and laptops to him.

He later returned to Guinea and used the donated items to develop his own business: the Nako Diabaté Centre. Aboubacar's company provided paid computer science and accounting courses. The quality of government-provided education in Guinea is substandard. The Nako Diabaté Centre, on the other hand, managed to provide affordable and accessible good-quality education in the capital, Conakry, as well as in some of the country's other cities. Students could take lessons on second-hand PCs that worked properly. His school was a real success. Over time, he also sold second-hand PCs and laptops from Belgium in Guinea, including to the Guinean government. He later expanded his activities to housing projects.

Incofin was one of the first to provide the Nako Diabaté Centre with a loan. When Guinea imposed a freeze on all foreign currency payments in 2004, Aboubacar personally travelled to Belgium to repay the interest owed on the loan. Under no circumstances did he want to default on his repayments. Today, Aboubacar's Nako Diabaté Centre is the largest training institute in Guinea.

The story of Aboubacar, with whom I became friends, illustrates the power of creativity and entrepreneurship. Aboubacar's short migration to Belgium also became a success story for both himself and Africa, perhaps the mirror image of the story about the Ethiopian migrants from the first chapter.

It is people like Aboubacar who personify the future of Africa. The continent may be facing a great deal of challenges, but I am convinced that the ubiquitous creativity of its young population justifies my immense optimism for the future.

I invite everyone to look beyond the impression of hopelessness that news reports about Africa can create to consider the continent's underlying dynamism and to also embrace it in all its fascinating diversity.

Note

1 B. Oyelaran-Oyeyinka, *Resurgent Africa: Structural Transformation in Sustainable Development.* Anthem Studies in Innovation and Development, Kindle Edition, 174.

INDEX

Page numbers in **bold** refer to figures in the text.

www.ingramcontent.com/pod-product-compliance
Lightning Source LLC
Chambersburg PA
CBHW020613270326
41927CB00005B/317